HOW
MUCH IS
ENOUGH?

How Much Is Enough?

Harness the Power of Your Money Story

Pamela York Klainer

BASIC
BOOKS

A Member of the Perseus Books Group

Published by Basic Books,
A Member of the Perseus Books Group

Designed by Bookcomp, Inc.

A cataloging-in-publication record for this book
is available from the Library of Congress.
ISBN 0-465-03748-8

02 03 04   10 9 8 7 6 5 4 3 2 1

For
Jerry, Sara, and Matt

And for those who have, at different critical stages in my life,
helped hone a writer's voice: Bern McCann, Dominga Batista,
Marie Cantlon, Kate Schroeder-Bruce, Laureen Connelly Rowland, and
Liz Maguire

CONTENTS

ACKNOWLEDGMENTS

MY FRIEND AND LEGAL COUNSEL Ralph Merzbach has observed that bringing a book to market more resembles its own small industry than a solitary creative pursuit. Ralph is exactly right. Many hands have touched this project, each adding in some crucial way to what the book has finally become.

Kate Schroeder-Bruce served as my sounding board on psychological issues in the book, and as a consultant to my Executive Coaching practice for many years before the book even began. My own perspective on human development is that of an educator and entrepreneur. As my consulting work with clients on issues of money, success, and happiness deepened, I also saw the work grow more psychological in nature. Underlying the psychological voice in all of my professional endeavors, and especially in this book, is Kate's wisdom, experience, keen insight, and generosity of spirit.

Karen Mackie has an uncommon mind. As a professional colleague and friend, Karen's willingness to sit with me, teasing out ideas and tinkering with what they might mean, has made me a sharper witness to our human story.

Dr. Melanie May and Reverend Rose Mitchell gave a more current context and depth to my somewhat dusty theological references. Judy Overholt, Laurie Dwyer, and Deb Mourey combed the Web for facts and details that I might have otherwise missed. Mary Ann Giglio, a lover of words, read the near-to-final draft with the eye of a craftsperson, so that the final text sent to Basic Books was as nearly perfect as could be.

Photographer Sigrid Estrada and stylist Pamela Jenrette helped create my "public face" for the book.

Later in the text you will read about "organizers" – those who specialize in building order out of chaos. Dawn Wiley is my organizer, the person who deals efficiently and imaginatively with everything I might otherwise worry about so that I can concentrate on writing.

A literary agent is the first "insider" in the publishing business who says, "Yes, there's a book here." Laureen Connelly Rowland is smart, direct, insightful, funny, and very, very skilled at guiding her authors through both the lofty and the mundane of creating a successful book.

A fine editor makes you sound more like yourself, only crisper and better. A fine editor also shows you how to take your very best effort and kick it up one final notch, like tackling the last 900 feet of Mt. Everest. Liz Maguire is that kind of editor. She and Laureen are also terrific companions for drinks, dinner, and a New York Liberty basketball game, and I'm grateful for that aspect of the writing life as well.

My extended family, friends, and professional colleagues have responded to this project with an eager "Here's how I can help," often before I even thought to ask.

Finally, I'm grateful to the people who so honestly shared their stories, and to my husband Jerry, daughter Sara, and son Matt – the three people I can always count on, and who are "enough" just as they are.

What's a Money Story, and Why Does Yours Matter?

THIS IS A MONEY BOOK, but not a book about earning, saving, investing, spending, or gifting. As a successful person, you most likely have the art of making money nailed. You intuitively grasp how to create value in the marketplace, and reap financial rewards for doing so. You're probably also fairly skilled at investing, at the art of making money from money, or have had the wisdom to hire financial advisors who are.

Instead, this is a book about your experience of money, as revealed through your money story. Talking about your experience of money is, at a very deep level, talking about you – where you came from, who you are now, what kind of person you ultimately want to be, what kind of relationships you value, and where you find meaning in life. Talking about your experience of money has everything to do with how you understand professional success, and with whether you can allow yourself to be happy. Your experience of money, with all its twists and turns and confusing aspects, reveals important truths that you may not discover anywhere else.

Where might you find such a story? You don't have to look far. Each of us has, in our private memories and public moments, all the components of a money story. That story – how we grew up with money, how we live with money now, and what we hope money will do for us in the future – has a lot to do with our happiness.

If you're like most of us, your relationship with money is better in some parts of your life than in others. If your money story isn't working for you across the board, you can change the parts that are giving you trouble. Changing your money story is a powerful tool for changing your life.

The first step is to figure out what your money story is.

The professor requests that students address her as "Doctor," which they are careful to do. Her mother's minimum wage job at the luncheonette commanded no such respect. The customers simply shouted "Hey Betty" when they wanted a refill on coffee, or the check.

The retired cardiologist says that he's always driven a nice car, but not the car he would have wanted, or could have afforded. "We lived in a mostly Christian neighborhood, and I worked at a Christian hospital. I didn't want them to think of me as the rich Jew."

The cabby darts through traffic and construction on the road from midtown Manhattan to JFK, grousing to himself. One hundred ten dollars to rent the cab, then twenty-five for gas, before he even gets to take a dollar home. A new baby coming, his first, due to arrive any day. The city fixed the return fare at $30.00, regardless of gridlocked morning traffic. It's a hard job, he mutters under his breath, a hard job to make any money.

We tend to focus more on other story threads in our lives, such as those that remind us where we came from and who we are. Most of us crave the details of our forebears coming to America, or the saga of how a feisty great-aunt or grandmother marched for women's suffrage, or the anecdote, told and retold among the family, of how a gesture we made "was just what your Dad would have done."

What we put into words about money reflects what's considered acceptable by our social group. For my fifty-fifth birthday I bought the car of my dreams, a sapphire blue Jaguar. My white, upper-middle-class friends commented extensively on the color, the interior, the hood ornament, but never on the price. My Latina friend Gladys was far more direct. "Aye, Pamela, que lindo! How much did it cost?"

Katherine, now a sixty-year-old architect, was raised lace-curtain Irish Catholic in a tony Boston suburb. Her mother always made clear that "a lady never talks openly about money." But architects must when they bid on jobs and negotiate contracts. Learning to be direct about money has been a long, and at times, painful struggle – one from which Katherine's mother always withheld recognition or approval.

Money stories have a long reach. They go back in time to our childhood; they go forward in time to affect our own children. Money stories remind us, often in jarring ways, how far we've traveled from our roots. When he was about ten, my son Matt accompanied me to Iowa for a reunion of my long-dead father's family. We stopped by the old folks' home to see my Aunt Ethel. When I was a child the family went to visit her and Uncle Alvin on the farm, where she cooked thick white sausage gravy over mashed potatoes for our dinner. This day Matt and I took her to lunch at the café in town, where we picked from among the hot homemade offerings like meat loaf and roast turkey with gravy. At the end of the meal Aunt Ethel opened her left hand, which had been clenched in a fist all through lunch. Out fell three wadded-up $5.00 bills. "If I can't cook for you any more, I'm going to pay for the lunch." Her tone was proud and pugnacious as she waved away my hand reaching for my wallet. Matt expected one of the grownups to simply whip out a credit card. From the look on his face he knew something important just happened, but seemed unsure what it might have been.

Families share a collective money story.

The daughter of inherited wealth grows tired of being watched and openly judged relative to the community's expectations of her prominent family. She will, she tells me, move far away to Washington, D.C. and start over. As her voice gains excitement with the possibilities she suddenly stops cold. "But if I do that I'll be a stranger, and just like everyone else. No one will know my name."

Companies, non-profits, faith communities, governmental bodies – all complex organizations – develop money stories that anchor the overall culture.

The founders of a software solutions company talked often and openly about the importance of a humane work environment, the level of interesting projects they would offer their employees, and the ways in which they valued people as their greatest asset. They remained silent about the rest: their goal of building the company to sell. Later successful in that goal, they were taken aback when the employees felt bitter and betrayed. "They were just like everyone else in this business," employees grumbled to each other. "It was all about the money."

Money stories – the telling of significant events from the perspective of money – can be tricky. Sometimes money stories remain entirely unspoken; people are expected to "just understand" the hidden messages. Sometimes what gets spoken is more about what money is not.

"Money isn't what motivates me."

"Money can't buy love, or happiness."

"Money can't buy good health, or keep your kids on the straight and narrow."

What Money Does Mean?

Defining what money means remains elusive. It's hard to pinpoint when we mull over who and what we've become, whether we're happy, whether the success we've finally attained is enough to allow us to stop piling up credits and still feel safe. The importance of money in those ongoing questions has not diminished. To the contrary, in our American culture money has moved to center stage and demands a "full spotlight" presence.

Money has gone well beyond its literal function as a way to provide for our essential needs and has become, in itself, an essential need. In a much more global sense than has been the case for previous generations, money marks our place in the world. We become what we earn. "I'm a six-figure person," a client considering a career change at a lesser income once said to me. "How can I possibly take that kind of a salary cut?" Professional success has also gone well beyond its historical role as an indicator of achievement or class status. Professional success has a much more global role in defining who and what we are. Consider introductions made even in casual or social settings: "I'd like you to meet Sharon; she's president of the Wolf Group." Consider the discomfort of people who are not working outside the home, or who have no professional tag line to add to their names. I'm sure you've felt the awkwardness, the sense of being without a place in the pecking order, when a person follows his or her introduction with: "Well, I don't really do anything interesting like you." In that sense professional success, like money, marks our place in the world. If there's a way in which we become what we earn, there's also a way in which we become what we do. To the extent that pursuing money and success are a consuming part of our everyday lives, both are major influences in shaping us.

Why does any of that matter? It matters because we're working harder and earning more – yet we continue to be driven, restless, unsatisfied. Money and success may not deliver on the goal of achieving happiness in quite the way we thought, yet we still follow that elusive path. It matters because many of the things we used to count on as moorings – extended family, neighborhoods, volunteering, participation in faith communities – no longer carry the same weight in helping us decide what counts. Money rushes into those gaps with a clear and simple standard. If it's big ticket, it's important. If not, why would you take it on?

You may be wondering if this is another work/life-balance book. The answer is: not exactly. Contemporary work/life-balance books, like Robert Reich's *The Future of Success*, argue that work needs to be balanced with "the rest of life." This book argues that for men and women vigorously pursuing money and success, work has become the rest of life, or at least the organizing center around which most other things – friendship, volunteer service, spirituality, and family needs – are set in place. I don't agree with Reich that most people would lead more balanced lives if they could. Many of the people you will read about in this book could, but choose not to.

Within what I will describe as the "culture of success," money is the chief marker of who we are and where we stand. As such, money is a unique window into who we really are, and a uniquely powerful leverage point in changing who we might become.

The economic boom that began in the early 1990s has left millions of us – especially those on the right side of the information-based economy – with more money than we had growing up, more money than many of us ever anticipated earning, and with significant professional success. Whether financial markets stumble or soar, the impact of money on our lives looms more important than ever. Talented, ambitious, and successful, we find ourselves mentally and physically exhausted, disconnected from people we profess to care about, and unable to shake the unrelenting drive to do more, think harder, work faster, with no end in sight.

This book urges you to step back and ask a vital question. Many of us absorbed the message that money and success do add up to happiness. In your experience, have they to the degree you had hoped? Or are you more likely to ask yourself these kinds of questions:

"Now that I don't have to worry about bills all the time, why aren't I happier?"

"Now that I'm financially secure, why am I so terrified when the market takes a dip? What gets re-awakened? "

"Now that I've made it and everyone can see that I've made it, why don't I feel better? Why can't I give myself permission to enjoy what I have?"

"Now that I've done everything professionally I said I wanted to do, why can't I stop?"

This is the money book for successful people seeking to move from anxiety and "the game of relentless pursuit" to lives that are connected, passionate, vibrant, and meaningful.

Getting Started

How do you embark on such a path? How do you go from the ordinary moments, where money is a casual or seemingly peripheral part of the conversation, to the "aha" moment that can drive real changes in your life?

Within the past few years I went day sailing on a forty-foot-long rented Hinckley, resplendent with brass and teak, whose purchase price new was in excess of $1 million. Two of my sailing companions were successful mid-life men: a surgeon with a high six-figure annual income, and a partner in a profitable money-management firm. They were casually bantering about the then free-floating Silicon Valley money, and its presumed negative effects on the young recipients. "How," they demanded of me," can we get someone to dump millions of bucks into our laps? Watch how long it would take us to get over the guilt, and really begin to be happy."

Their banter turned toward me because of my profession: I'm a workplace consultant, primarily to leaders in entrepreneurial business and to fast-track corporate executives paid hefty six-figure incomes to handle turnaround or rapid growth. Money issues loom large in these settings, both on the business and the personal side. Indeed, one of the earliest questions clients ask me, often in the midst of mulling over one strategic business decision or another, is this: "If I have all this money and professional challenge, why don't I feel better? Why aren't I happier? Why aren't I having more fun?"

Beneath their banter about doing the Silicon Valley types one better, my companions were headed straight for a familiar theme. That theme, which I explore so often in my consulting practice, is the longing of successful people who have worked hard for two or three decades to have had the money come more easily, with less personal cost, and with the elusive "happiness and a sense of meaning" in tow.

Money conversation in our culture doesn't usually go beyond banter. Here is the point at which, if we were following conventional social norms, the conversation would have veered off into jokes about flaky young millionaires, or about shrinks who make a living dissecting the guilt felt by the worried wealthy. Instead, I took the conversation seriously, and invited my companions to do the same. I responded by asking them to dig deeper with their questions.

"You already have money. You also know perfectly well how to ratchet up your income and multiply your assets if you want to. What would be different if you were richer? Would you rent the boat for a longer time, or rent a bigger boat, or buy your own Hinckley? Would you drive to the dock in a classier car? Would you each buy a third home? Why do you think having more money would make you any happier?"

They paused for a long moment, mulling over my questions, before they were rescued by an abrupt change of wind. Skilled hands, they leapt to deal with the suddenly flapping sails. Because they were companions, not clients, and because the day was meant for relaxation, I held back from pushing further. One of the men has a young teenage daughter who suffers from a severe developmental disability. Money has bought her the finest in residential care, but not wellness. In your quest for happiness as it relates to your daughter, I could have asked him, what might more money accomplish? Would it bring you closer to her? Would it give you more time to spend with her? Would you let money do that, or would you use seeking more money as a reason to escape the pain of her limitations? The other man is married to a woman who was once comatose for several weeks following a stroke; she did not join us on the sail. Her recovery from brain trauma, while substantial, has been painstakingly won over a period of many years. A day on the shifting deck of a fast-moving boat might overtax her balance, dexterity, and ability to manage stress. And what, I might ask him, does more money have to do with that? Do you really think more money will make you happier than you are now?

Finally Getting Honest

Hidden in plain sight, our beliefs and resulting behavior around money have everything to do with who we are. Why do we avoid exploring that money experience? The avoidance is often expressed in ways like this: "I want you to know the reason I work 50, 60, 80 hours a week isn't about the money. First and foremost, it's about keeping score. It's also about shaping the global story of my industry, and making a big footprint on the world. It's about staying challenged, staying sharp, staying at the top of my game. It's about being a player, and having everyone know I'm a player."

People in helping professions, such as academics and public servants, say a similar thing, but in a different way. "I want you to know the reason I work 50, 60, or 80 hours a week isn't about the money. In fact, money isn't important to me at all. What's important to me are social issues and making the world a better place. In fact, asking for more money is hard for me. I want my work to be about people [or ideas, or service to others, or whatever]. When I ask for more money – even when I really need the salary increase – it taints my convictions about what kind of person I am."

In our fervent denial of the role money plays in our lives, we protest too much. What we do 50, 60, or 80 hours a week is, at a very deep level, what our lives are about. That's what I mean when I say "we become what we do." If we spend that amount of time on activities that generate money – working, doing research, serving others in a helping profession, creating art that we sell to make a living – then our lives as successful people are, at a very deep level, about our experience of money. That's true whether we pursue money, avoid it, or proclaim it as secondary to professional satisfaction. That's true whether we make a lot of money, or an average amount. In my view, choices about money – reflecting our experience of money, not our investing prowess – are primary story threads in our lives. That doesn't mean we're a re-issued version of the 1980's barbarians at the gate. It doesn't mean we're fast-moving vultures looking to strip bare the opportunities our less-successful competitors have left by the wayside. It doesn't mean we're addicted consumers, high-flying gamblers, or socially uncommitted narcissists. What it does mean is considerably more subtle.

People who work for most of their waking hours – with some extra time built into the day for exercise, eating, travel to and from the office or lecture hall or client site – aren't doing much else. For all the buzz about work/life balance, there isn't much balance in a ten- or twelve- or fourteen-hour workday. At most, we carefully allocate time for work, immediate family, keeping up with the latest technology, monitoring our investment portfolio, and exercising. That means social practices that used to give us a richly textured sense of reality – visiting with extended family, being a real part of a neighborhood, joining local political or service organizations or volunteer opportunities, attending religious services – recede in importance.

As those traditional practices have taken on a diminished role, the importance of work and money has greatly expanded. To the extent that's true for large numbers of people, then examining the pursuit of money can be a dramatic way to illuminate who we really are, and what really makes us happy.

I choose the word "illuminate" deliberately, to suggest shining light on or making conscious those things that may be lurking in the background of our daily awareness. With consciousness can come intention. What you can speak about and understand, you can learn from. You can use that learning to change behavior patterns that have left you tense and unsatisfied, and begin to make choices about money that fit better with your deepest beliefs and values. That's what I mean when I say later in the book, "Surprise, surprise, it really is about the money."

Where Can the Honesty Lead?

How can you tap that previously unexplored reservoir of information? How will your money story take shape and point you in new directions? It's not as hard as you may think. The watchwords, quite simply, are "follow the money." Instead of veering off just when the money conversation gets interesting, discipline yourself to go against social norms by going deeper. You've learned to talk about other difficult matters: safe sex, abortion politics, the influence of religious groups in national elections. All of these, once taboo subjects in polite society – have become part of responsible adult conversation. Plain talk about your experience of money remains the last taboo, and one that needs to be broken. Follow the money, and see where the narrative leads you. The rewards, in terms of insight and the opportunity for change, can be substantial.

In the following chapters I'm going to show you how to understand your money story. Then I'm going to open up a number of questions that are implicit in money choices we face every day, yet are rarely openly discussed:

How do you manage the power of money? Can you do it without riding roughshod over other people's preferences, desires, and aspirations?

Do you see yourself as a provider, or as an organizer? How do you negotiate ownership of those roles at home and in the workplace?

Do you see money as for "me" or for "we"? If it's for "me", how do you create a larger sense of meaning about your life? If you see your money as having a larger social purpose, how do you act on that in any intelligent way when what you mostly do is work?

How do you handle the complications of money decisions, the times when you're not sure whether your course of action is right, wrong, or painfully relative?

How much is enough? What do you care about beyond amassing money and professional recognition? If you don't focus much on money, if you never ask yourself how much is enough, what are you missing?

We're going to dig into a range of responses to these questions, looking for patterns and larger truths. In each chapter I'm going to try to lighten the moment; money often evokes huge emotional reactions, sometimes anxiety and distress as well as exhilaration. When you've gone as far as you can with a given question, you get to stop and move on to another one. This is a book you can come back to again and again, as your sophistication in dealing with money's hardest questions grows. When you do get a flash of insight – what I call an "aha" moment – I'll suggest behavioral changes that will allow you to incorporate the insight into your daily life. The goal of the book is not only insight and wisdom, but change. In order to be different, in order to feel happier than you are now, you have to act differently in relation to your own success and to your money.

Your reward, at the end, will be a new resolution of the money + success = happiness equation. In ways that are simple yet dramatic, that can mean a new you. One young provider uncharacteristically stepped out of his role as "good soldier," willing to take on all the problem areas of the company without being financially rewarded. He boldly risked initiating a salary negotiation, trusting that he delivered more value than he had previously claimed. In another case, a rising star just offered a plum job insisted on a sabbatical first, knowing that if this offer couldn't linger her talent would prompt another. In yet another case, the newly promoted corporate vice president quietly but firmly told her husband that in the case of their immediate professional conflict, her deliverable had to come first and he had to forego his business trip and manage the kids.

"A new you" means being able to say this: "I've not seen myself this way before nor been able to act accordingly. Now that I can, I'm much happier."

Linking Your Story with Mine

Of all the story threads on which a workplace consultant might focus, why do I zero in on money? Like other consultants, I work with individual leaders, high-level teams, and workplace culture. All involve meaty, substantive issues that give rise to powerful stories of their own.

Those issues are matters of the head – things that can be left in a briefcase without a second thought and taken out again the next day. Losing $400,000 on a failed hydropower investment back in the 1980s – what my husband and I now refer to as "the damned dam" – was not a matter of the head. For me, it was like being dropped into the middle of an icy lake, so cold it seared my lungs and left me gasping for breath. And yet the loss made no real difference in my day-to-day life, nor in that of my family.

How can $400,000 vanish, with only pride and business judgment taking any real hit? The question refused to stay in my briefcase. During the day I very rationally coped, managed, decided about a whole host of things. At night, I struggled over what it meant to have enough money so that the loss of $400,000 didn't make any noticeable difference.

The investment loss and the lack of an aftermath meant I am a rich woman. I have enough money, in my own right and in my own name, to stop working if I chose to and live on the income from my assets. Taking into account joint assets, my husband and I could both live very well without working another day, and have money left to leave to our adult son and daughter. Yet neither of us ever uses the word "rich" when we talk or think about ourselves.

Neither of us really thinks of a time when we will not be working. The reason, we say, is that we love what we do. That's true, but only part of the truth.

I was not always rich. My father worked as a supervisor in a chemical plant; my mother was a homemaker. My father died suddenly at 49, when I was 14. My mother returned to work as a secretary. My sisters and I are rare among our cousins in having gone to college; among the three of us, we have two doctoral degrees and five masters' degrees. Our New Jersey cousins are cops in Jersey City, firemen in Newark, toll collectors on the Garden State Parkway. Our Midwestern cousins all left the farms on which they grew up and could no longer make a living. My cousin Colleen became a hairdresser; she and her husband Louis operated the two-seat "Graves the Great Hair Salon" on a side street off the town square in Bloomfield, Iowa.

Consciously and deliberately, I left home and became who I am now. Over a recent summer I saw my cousin Bobby at a family wedding. Close as families growing up, he and I hadn't seen each other in 35 years. His first words to me were stark. "You left town and never came back. Where did you go?"

What threads of your own story keep you up at night because they're hard to sort out and hard to reconcile? Which of those threads has something important – now that you think of it – to do with money? Together, we'll see where the money threads lead. That's the story, for most of us, the least told.

I write as a reflective practitioner, not as a researcher on workplace issues, a psychologist treating clinical conditions that can arise in relation to money, or as a social scientist interested in the behavior of individuals or groups. Most commonly, I tell the tale using short vignettes from my actual work with thousands of people over a period of ten years, plus snippets of my own story. Those vignettes bring the money story to life, in all its texture and complexity, in a way statistics alone never could. The vignettes are about people from across the country who have made dramatic shifts in the way they work, earn, and play. They are perhaps like you and me – successful people, financially secure, who stayed awake at night longing for things to fall into place and craving something more.

The vignettes are real people and real situations, not composites. I use these individual examples in the manner of a memoirist, in the sense that any individual life can be symbolic of larger human truths. In some cases, because people have asked for privacy, I've disguised their names and actual work situations.

The stories you will read here are about ordinary, not famous people. That's a deliberate choice, reflecting my belief that money is an ordinary issue. "Ordinary" means that everyone can gain access to the wisdom and self-knowledge that delving into money can provide. With wisdom and self-knowledge can come change. At stake is your own answer to the question of why you work so hard and still find happiness elusive. At stake is the chance to let money and success – now, if never before – really illuminate the path to happiness.

CHAPTER ONE

Your Money Story: How You Juggle "Money + Success = Happiness"

JOAN'S STORY IS ABOUT a turbulent beginning, a hot burner, a seven-figure net worth, and a deep, unmet yearning. Joan and I began working together in 1996. At the time she was one of three principals in a technology firm that had been founded in 1993 and was growing by leaps and bounds. She worked long hours, often putting in extended time even on the weekends. She and her husband of ten years juggled a bicoastal marriage, with her company located on the West Coast and his employment remaining on the East Coast. Hearing of my work with successful but exhausted leaders, she arrived at her first appointment with a question:

> "If I have all this money, why aren't I happy?" Her voice – so clear and commanding when she had called to make the appointment – now sounded tired and sad. "I feel as if my hand is on a hot burner and I can't pull it away, even though I know I'm being hurt. This isn't what I imagined success would be like."

Somewhere along the line, many of us who are professionally successful got the message that our financial security and workplace achievements, in and of themselves, should add up to happiness.

Certain questions that bedevil my clients have a simpler answer than how money and success equate with happiness. These simpler questions can usually be resolved within a limited time frame. The person reviews the issues, comes to a decision, and moves on with his or her life. The questions sound like this: "My company just revised the commission schedule in a way that doesn't favor me. Should I stay or go?" Or, "I do the behind-the-scenes organizing work that keeps projects on schedule and clients happy. How can I get paid better for that, when my company only seems to reward the big personality people out securing clients in the first place?"

Joan's question was of a different kind, deeper and more complex. Hers is not the kind of concern from which one easily "moves on." Her question sounds like this: "I'm successful at what I thought counted the most for making my life happy and meaningful. Along with my partners, I've launched and operated a profitable business that runs according to the cultural values we've instilled. We've all made good money at it. I have a much bigger range of choices in my life now, and I'm only 38. Why do I feel so terrible?"

As time unfolded, Joan showed her seriousness about this question and her willingness to commit time and energy – her scarcest resources – to resolving it. She's exceedingly bright and fiery in her passion about the company and the culture she and her partners are creating. By contrast, she's coolly logical and unsentimental about even the hardest business decisions. Perhaps surprisingly for a person beset by so many distracting demands, she is deeply creative, artistic, and spiritual. She's one of a small handful of clients who described our work together from the very beginning as a "spiritual practice." By that, she was asking me to help her beleaguered spirit decide where it wanted to go.

Like many successful people, Joan had made her work the hub, the central organizing factor, in her busy life. Work claimed the first passionate energy of the morning and often the last gasp of coherence at the end of the day. Everything else had to fit in around, under, or between.

In many ways, Joan's situation is emblematic of a whole cohort of bright, highly educated, talented, and successful people, who find themselves in a place vastly different from where they grew up and where they now expected to be. Those differences make the search for happiness more convoluted than was the case for our parents' generation, and the generations before.

The Changes

In today's economic environment, a larger share of the population has money than was true thirty years ago. Every ten years the Census Bureau collects extensive data about the population of the United States, including financial information. That "every ten year look" provides an ongoing set of reference points that track our collective financial progress. Despite stock market ups and downs over the past thirty years, the most recent U.S. Census Bureau data show that the top 40% of this country's income-earning households have made real and substantial financial gains during that period.

As a child in the early 1950s, I remember my father bringing home his weekly pay in cash. My mother then distributed the fives, tens, and twenties among a series of manila budgeting envelopes marked with the basics: mortgage, gas and electric, food, clothing, telephone. There was no envelope marked "investments." We did "Christmas Club" at our local savings and loan, which was a non-interest-bearing account where we would save fifty cents or a dollar most weeks in order to accumulate enough money for holiday gifts. I'm not sure my parents even had a regular savings account during those years. If so, I imagine they simply saved at low-interest rates, never scraping together enough to buy even a certificate of deposit.

Joan's father left home after eighteen years of marriage to her mother, who made out badly in the divorce. High school educated, her mother finally was awarded only five years of alimony from her college-professor husband. The roots of what we think will make our lives happy and meaningful typically go back a long way. Surely in Joan's case – and no doubt in mine – the choice never to be economically vulnerable, especially to the degree our mothers were, drives at least part of our intensity about money.

With additional money comes choice, and with choice comes greater complexity. Through hard work, resiliency, and share of good fortune, both Joan and I have joined the ranks of what author Dinesh D'Souza calls the first mass affluent class in history. We have, as Joan pointed out, a much broader range of choices than was the case for our own parents and for previous generations. With choice comes awareness of limits; we can garner some good things in our lives, but not all. With choice comes accountability; some directions we pursue will have a better outcome than others. With choice comes responsibility; what we do affects not only our own lives, but the lives of others, the physical space we inhabit, and the hope we are able to sustain for the future.

My mother is now 87. In what I think of as a very Irish Catholic way, she relishes going over the minute details of her funeral plans, writing and rewriting her obituary, even determining where we are all to go out to eat after the cemetery. About her epitaph she is very clear. "I want to be known as a person who did the best I could with what I had." In all my years of working with clients, I've never heard anyone else sum up the meaning of his or her life quite that simply. For those of us deep in the throes of "relentless pursuit," the epitaph is more likely to be "I wanted to know for sure if I was there yet."

Not only is there lots of new money around, but people are gaining access to big money at a much younger age. Knowing what happiness means requires a certain wisdom reflective of life experience. People who are relatively young in accumulating that wisdom can be at a marked disadvantage. Joan and her partners all achieved a seven-figure net worth in their late 30's and early 40's. Lest you think such relatively early affluence is purely a Silicon Valley, Denver, Boston, or Research Triangle phenomenon, it isn't. I can bring you back East to an ordinary mid-sized city, where the three male partners of a technology firm are also in their 30's and early 40's. This company is at an earlier point in its growth curve than Joan's, but the founders' exit strategy as millionaires is no more than three or four years away. I can take you to a New England medical practice, where the founding partner has been extremely innovative about making the managed care reimbursement system work in his favor, and that of his patients. I can take you to a

Midwestern urban hub, where a young consultant with a six-figure income, a willingness to travel for new career-building projects, and frugal habits is well on the way to the coveted "first million."

As you examine your own situation, you may well find yourself with substantial income and assets at a relatively young age, in good health, and with the rest of your life ahead. ("Relatively young age" is, of course, relative. Actress Tyne Daly and I are about the same age. I consider myself still on the upswing of middle age. Daly, by contrast, is reported to see herself as "an apprentice old lady.") Deciding what constitutes "happiness," in my view, takes the perspective of life experience and a degree of reflective wisdom. Hitting the jackpot on money and success early in life can create certain dislocations in that process.

One of the dislocations has to do with speed. I got my first car loan in 1969, when I was 24 and had just returned from the Peace Corps. I bought a used Nash Rambler with a lot of miles on it. Over the years I worked my way up through a new Plymouth Duster, a Volkswagen squareback, a Chevy wagon, a Volvo, a used Lexus with low mileage, and now the Jaguar. My daughter Sara, at age 25, drives a classy new Saab with tight handling on curves, a leather interior, and lots of options. My son Matt, 23, drives a fast new Jetta, with a lighted dashboard panel that looks like a racing car or hot aircraft. Both bought their cars outright with their earned money, not by tapping the assets that have been gifted to them. Both were careful in deciding how much to spend, how much car was enough. Matt bought a Jetta, not the Passat, because he said that at his age he simply didn't need the more upscale model.

I look on with awe as my daughter and son make big financial decisions, and in a far more sophisticated manner than I did at their age. I also wonder, having gotten to the "great car" point so fast, where do they go from here?

Another dislocation – especially in the early career-building stage – has to do with the value of "doing" over "being." Simply being with one's experience and taking the time to sort out what it means is the essence of reflective wisdom. At a recent conference I shared coffee-break conversation with a fellow speaker whose job it is to build the ecommerce business of a major U.S. automaker. He was clearly younger than I am, perhaps 35 or so. As he described his relentless schedule of travel, high-level meetings, and intense turf-war negotiations, I asked when he had time to reflect on the longer-term strategy that would sustain his business over time. His response was both incredulous and impatient. "I have no time to reflect."

As big money comes at younger ages, profound life questions that used to arise in midlife come much earlier. A 2001 *New York Times* article profiled the difficulties that can now confront people barely out of college. Questions like "What's next for me?" and "Is this all there is?", long the staples of the mid-50's life crisis, are now being asked by seemingly jaded 25-year-olds. With such limited life experience, they have slim pickings from which to find good answers to such hard questions.

Along with the opportunity to earn big money comes a reduction in the range of things successful people do. Mostly, they work. It's all too easy, then, to arrive at the conclusion that whatever happiness one might find in life has to have its origins at work. Getting a work-related email from Joan that was sent at 3 A.M. is not unusual. When my consulting practice first went national, I relished the time difference between the East Coast and California. Then I had to remind myself that the three-hour window didn't automatically mean extending my workday from eight hours to eleven hours, just because I could easily reach West Coast people at 8 P.M. and beyond.

The head of the emergency room medical practice and his staff physicians all worked twelve-hour shifts three days a week, for efficiency of scheduling. That, along with adjunct teaching at a prominent medical school, supervising residents, staying on top of the managed care bills in the legislature, attending statewide professional meetings, and completing continuing education requirements, made him an "early to bed" kind of guy.

The Chicago-based consultant boards a plane Sunday afternoon or evening to arrive at her project site fresh for work on Monday. Fourteen-hour days are the norm. Late Thursday night she jets back to O'Hare, to be available in the home office for staff meetings and project updates on Friday. Exhausted by Friday night, she crashes early. Her down time is Saturday morning through Sunday mid-afternoon. She cooks, works out, picks up her dry cleaning, waters plants, pays bills, and goes grocery shopping. I ask about friends and other diversions. "Of course, I have lots of friends. We email each other all the time."

The findings of Robert D. Putnam's *Bowling Alone* are now widely known: the locally based social and service endeavors that used to create social capital have seen a steep decline in membership. Sociologist Alan Wolfe observes similar trends, but comes to a less pessimistic conclusion. Wolfe believes we're still building human connections, albeit in different ways. My own position is closer to Wolfe's. I think we're in a transitional period of understanding what new forms of community are evolving. Often, those new forms seem to originate at work. People volunteer in the community as part of company-sponsored teams. We wave to our neighbors, but the annual picnic is more likely to be a departmental function than a block party. When we meet up at the end of the day for a bite to eat and a movie, it's often with people we've already spent much of the day with at work.

When people had a range of important experiences with different people on a daily basis, they had a number of ways to feel successful and happy with their accomplishments. Someone with a tedious supervisory job might achieve considerably more stature and satisfaction being a local ward captain, a church elder or temple president, or the organizer of a powerful neighborhood association. Someone with a limited and easily overlooked work role might be a pivotal and much-loved person in an extended family, the one to whom everyone looks for guidance, emotional connection, and support.

When people mostly work, feelings of success and satisfaction are heavily dependent on one's fortunes in the workplace. That's a far more limited field of experience than was available to previous generations.

Not only do a lot of people have more money and work more, but the very definition of "happiness" seems to have changed. For a large segment of the post-Depression and post–World War II working population, "being happy" meant having good health, stable family relationships, and enough money to pay the bills and take a short vacation once a year.

In New Jersey, where I grew up in the 1950s, "being happy" meant being "down the shore," renting a bungalow at a beachfront community for a week or two. That the refrigerator was, in fact, an icebox and the toilet was outside the bungalow made little difference; we got to swim every day. During alternate summers, we'd drive to Iowa to visit my father's family on their farms. My father always drove an Oldsmobile. On those trips, he seemed really happy and proud to be going back to Iowa in a shiny, new-looking car that signaled to everyone how well he was doing. As higher education became more accessible to middle- and working-class families, having the money to send kids to college became an added expectation. These basic accomplishments have, in our current culture, been supplanted by the constant "adrenaline high" of the wired workplace and the demand that we put productivity first. Having time to mentor a new employee, read a long book, or watch a kid's entire soccer game has vanished in favor of multitasking and making every minute count. We sit on the sidelines of our children's games, tapping away on our hand-held email devices or our super-thin laptops, only looking up when the noise level signals something about to happen. We miss a lot. Clearly, a new element has been added to the definition of "happiness": making a big and visible footprint on the world. My daughter Sara has always had a wandering spirit. Since graduating from Tufts she has worked in the travel industry. During her first year, she was the company's second-highest producer in the whole United States. In 2000, her goal was not only to be #1, but the biggest #1 the company ever had. She blasted through the existing bonus structure; they had to create a new one to recognize her level of production. She and other high producers were sent off to Peru at company expense to celebrate their accomplishments.

An often-unstated factor in our difficulty sorting out money, success, and happiness is the loss of moorings that used to come from organized religious practice. Joan is no longer part of the mainline Protestant denomination in which she was raised. She's attracted to the beliefs and practices of Buddhism, particularly the spiritual principle of "detachment." She has a small chant room in her home, large enough for one person, in which she has meditation tapes, incense, and objects that carry spiritual meaning for her.

The Jewish physician often hosts a seder in the springtime for his extended family. In honor of family members' extensive intermarriage with Christian spouses – including his own – the traditional seder plate often includes a brightly colored Easter egg or two. The older generation, all Conservative or Orthodox Jews for whom seder was a formal religious ritual, would have been scandalized. No one in the current generation seems to care.

My sisters and I attended public schools through high school, then I chose a Catholic women's college to learn more about religious beliefs that had grounded the rituals of my childhood. Along the way, I discovered existentialist philosophy and Harvey Cox's book *The Secular City*, which told me I could go to the big city and be what I wanted, leaving behind the limitations of what I already knew. I graduated from both college and the practice of organized religion simultaneously.

In our current work-oriented culture, the place where people explore life's deepest meaning or life's defining purpose seems to have shifted from faith communities to workplaces. High on the list of spiritual challenges is the attempt to create business cultures where profitability, a humane environment, and personal fulfillment can all flourish.

The questions of ultimate meaning and what tempers a win-at-all-costs mentality have traditionally been the moral and ethical domains of organized religion. The questions of what product or service, how to make operational, how profitable, and how accountable have traditionally been in the domain of workplaces. Workplaces, in my view, have little expertise in dealing with questions of "should" or "ought," and as yet do a relatively poor job of setting boundaries on those kinds of questions. In the worst case, we find what author Paulina Borsook calls "philosophical techno-libertarianism," the belief system of those Silicon Valley high-fliers who are unable to reconcile the demands of personal satisfaction with the demands of living in society with other people.

The focus on work and money occurs at the epicenter of the change in gender roles that has only gained steam over the past thirty years. If Stanley and Danko's millionaires next door are predominately 55-year-old white males, it's also true that women in their 40's and 50's represent the first generations to be widely in the job market, earning professional salaries and with financial independence in their own right. As more women jump eagerly into the traditionally male role of "provider," the tongue-in-cheek cry of "I need a wife" – someone to organize home, children, and workplace – becomes an equal opportunity lament.

Most successful people, even those who are highly sophisticated at invest-ing money, still can't talk about money's powerful symbolic meaning.

Money has a literal meaning: it's the currency through which we buy and sell goods and services, pay the bills, and keep a roof over our heads. Money also has a symbolic meaning. A symbol is an object or an act that "stands in" for something else. When we use money as a way of "keeping score," we're using money in a symbolic sense. That means we're using money as a marker, or as a way of designating our perceived success relative to others.

When's the last time you had an honest conversation about the way you and your peers use money to keep score?

Many otherwise sophisticated and competent adults have a psy-chological framework around money that is comprised of a jumble of early and unexamined messages, metaphors, and partial mean-ings. To the extent that our early frameworks remain unspoken and unexplored, we remain ill-equipped to cope with the complex chal-lenge money always presents.

The Way We Live Now

My observation of the way we live now, having been buffeted by these changes to a greater or lesser degree, could apply to Joan's company, or to the Eastern software solutions group, or to the Chicago office of the consulting firm. It could apply to my son's dot.com or to my daughter's travel company.

Quite possibly, elements of the description apply to you.

What I've been calling "professionally successful people" probably have a family income of $40,000 to $75,000 at the low end and six figures or more at the high end. We're savers as well as spenders, and might well have assets in the $250,000 to $300,000 range or more. "More" could mean much more, into the millions. We consider ourselves professionals, although "professional" can mean teacher, cop, and electrician as well as criminal defense lawyer, brain surgeon, or merger and acquisition specialist. We're likely to have a college education, and perhaps advanced degrees. We're on-line for a considerable chunk of time each day, and use technology for more than checking email. We have high aspirations and even higher expectations of ourselves. We care how others see us. We can be as young as early 20's or as old as late 60's. If we are one of those Renaissance individuals who has never stopped learning and growing, we could be even older.

Perhaps surprisingly, only a small segment of us are 20-something technology geeks who spend most of the day in front of a computer, have already blown $12 million in venture capital, and wonder why we're lonely and how we can meet people without shutting off the glowing screen.

We work hard to keep ourselves at the cutting edge, yet we know that as fast as we add new skill sets, the performance bar keeps going up. We speak in jargon, like "brain dump" and "value add." Whether or not we have a naturally risk-taking temperament, we act outwardly as if we crave speed, sudden change, opportunities to show initiative, and jumping before all the pieces are locked down so we can be sure to be among the first. We know that "doing something that will get you reasonably close" is valued over "waiting until you understand the problem in depth and really have the resources to move." On rare breaks during the workday, we drink expensive coffee. We might have come to work in a vehicle that has the power to trek across Africa and is priced accordingly, yet we wear business casual instead of Armani. We want to be stars, but not "suits." We want power and influence, yet don't want to be seen as selling out. We want our power to come from being more brilliant and creative than anyone else, not because of formal position or title. We want others to follow us willingly because we're the best, not because of our authority to demand compliance. We want our power to be visible and recognized. We want flash. Our benchmarks are Bill Gates on market dominance and Steve Jobs on creative design, not the patrician David Rockefeller or legendary 1940s New York power broker Robert Moses. Our benchmarks are Carly Fiorina on rapid career advancement and Andrea Jung on being a savvy CEO/mom, not early corporate leader Estee Lauder or Washington political hostess turned ambassador Pamela Harriman. Perhaps most of all, we like to keep moving. We fidget. We change jobs. We change cities. We change friends. We see happiness as elusive, as something always moving away from us that we have to pursue with great intensity and drive.

Who Really Lives Like That?

In 1999 I was a speaker at a *Fast Company* Real Time Gathering. At that time *Fast Company,* a hefty monthly magazine often running to 400 or more pages, was the bible of the new workplace: fast, edgy, and influential. Filled with stories about success in the new economy and packed with ads for pricey goods and services, *Fast Company* clearly positioned itself to attract readers from the culture of success. Before arriving at the conference, I expected the majority of attendees to be young, buffed, affluent, and in the workforce more as free agents than as employees concerned about loyalty and career paths. When I found was quite different. Most participants were men and women in their 30's, 40's, and 50's who worked for more "bricks than clicks" companies like Target and Ford, not the 20-something dot.commers I had expected. Some were athletic and buffed; more had the body shapes of the fairly sedentary. Most had families and obligations; they did care about things like loyalty and career paths. Those who revealed income figures during my presentation were more in the $40,000 to $100,000 range, not the stunning mid-six and low seven figures of the dot.com winners.

So who really lives in the culture of success as I have described it? We do.

Do You Live Like That?

The important thing for locating your place in the world of successful people is not how literally your life maps with my description. The important thing is how the image of that culture of success, whether literally true or not, has influenced your life, your workplace, the expectations that are placed on you.

Are you expected to move faster, with fewer resources and less mentoring, than was the case when you started your career?

Does your chosen profession – academic, clergyperson, general practitioner, social worker – carry less status than it used to because what you do isn't trendy and doesn't rate really big money?

Is your organization quicker to jettison people who can no longer keep up with the pack, even if they've given twenty or more years of loyal and productive service?

Have you ever been expected to do anything like travel for thirty hours to a global marketing meeting in Asia, then be on deck at 8 A.M. fully alert and ready for an all-day strategy session?

Welcome to the spillover from the culture of success.

The culture of success is certainly home base for Joan. Five years after she and I began to work together, she came to my office with her husband. They were, she said, at a turning point. Joan was exploring a big promotion, one that would involve increased travel and much greater intensity than even her current role. She and her husband were still living in two cities, although now they at least lived in the same state and could be together for the weekend with a mere one-hour plane ride.

Despite having racked up more professional credits and more financial security than when we first met, Joan still had a deep, unmet longing and a sense that the work she loved was also in some ways destructive to her spirit.

On a white board in my office, I wrote the following in large letters:

MONEY + SUCCESS = HAPPINESS

I then told Joan and her husband we were going to have what she irreverently but graphically calls "a come to Jesus moment." That means a moment in which we strip away every bit of spin, and get dead honest.

First, I asked them to tell me their net worth, to say out loud the most accurate number they could come up with without taking time to review their financial statements. With some self-consciousness, they did. Part of the difficulty we all have in dealing with money is that we don't use numbers – we use euphemisms, like "a big win" or "comfortable" or "pretty well off." Using the actual number makes a difference, because it makes our assets tangible. I then asked if the income from that number – assuming a diversified, carefully moni-tored portfolio – was enough for them to live on, even if neither worked another day.

They waffled. "Can't the money go away if the stock market really tanks?" "Shouldn't we really have more before we think about whether we could live on the income or not?" "How can we be so cocky as to think about not working, when neither of us grew up that way? Isn't that tempting fate?"

They sat for a long time, staring at the seven-figure number I had written on the board above the word "money." Finally, calmly, they said what was obvious. "It's enough."

Do you know the number that will allow you to continue your lifestyle throughout your projected life expectancy? If not, there are financial advisors or off-the-shelf software packages aplenty that can help you figure it out. In whatever form you prefer, take the time to do this analysis. It's immensely powerful to have an actual number in front of you.

I then asked Joan to focus on the word "success." I pointed out that, along with her partners, she had founded a company, run it according to her values, done great work for clients, sold the company and had its value affirmed in the marketplace, grown into a skilled executive in the larger corporate network, and been offered an even bigger, more complex position. I suggested to her that professional success doesn't get any better than that, and she agreed. Whatever else she might choose to do, she's already "there" in terms of success.

You can replicate this part of the process by writing down what you think "success" in your chosen field means – to *you*, not to your parents, your spouse, your boss, the cohort of colleagues with whom you compete most directly, or your most critical and demanding friend. Then, ask yourself honestly how on track you are toward achieving that success. It's not an age thing, or a "years in the business" thing. Some people achieve success at a startlingly early point.

Finally, I moved to the word "happiness." Joan and her husband both agreed that happiness remained elusive in their stress-filled and demanding lives.

And you? Without making things too complicated and reflective, are you basically happy? Do you long to be happier than you are?

Pointing again to the whole equation, I asked: "If you take the new job, which side of the equation will be enhanced: the money and success side, or the happiness side?"

They both said, without prompting, "the money and success side." These are very bright people, and the light began to dawn. Joan spoke first. "I've already done that side, haven't I?"

I agreed. "You could focus on racking up more money and more success, but why? You already know how to do that. The interesting challenge now is to focus on what you don't know how to do so well, which is to find ways to let yourself be happy."

Certain moments in a long consulting relationship stand out from all other moments. Those are the times when something that has been shrouded in mystery suddenly becomes clear enough to touch. Such moments are palpable; you can literally feel them unfolding. They generally cannot be forced. They come when the person is ready to have them come. In Joan's case, this breakthrough took five grueling years. When it did come, Joan and her husband very rapidly made a series of crucial life decisions.

After some further conversation and within a matter of weeks, Joan and her husband agreed that they wanted to live in the same place, literally for the first time in their marriage. Since her work is the more portable, that meant consolidating two homes into one and relocating to the city where he is employed. She also decided to decline the job offer and instead, take a one-year unpaid sabbatical during which she would allow her spirit to roam. She and her husband planned to work with their financial advisor to arrange their assets so they would have a stream of income during the sabbatical, a replacement for the large salary she had been bringing in. After the year, she would return to work she loved.

What's the Point?

The point is to use this story to clarify what money and success do well, and what they really don't do at all, then to figure out how you can apply that wisdom to your own life.

The point is not that you should chuck what you're doing, become an entrepreneur, earn a few million dollars, then take a sabbatical. The point is to figure out how money and success play out for you, and what they have to do with your happiness.

In my view, money does two really big things. First, money buys breathing room. When you have to work every waking moment to put food on the table and pay the heat and light bills, you don't have a choice about taking your hand off the hot burner. You're stuck. That's something to think about – ahead of time – if you are a young person or a person returning to the marketplace who feels drawn to a low-paying occupation. If you choose low-paying work, or if you're in low-paying work and you choose to stay there, you'll never have much breathing room.

The second important insight is that money buys "containers" – things that you get to fill with your own sense of meaning. In Joan's case, the container is the sabbatical. What the sabbatical means to Joan is a chance to let her spirit rediscover its roots.

Be careful to note that the container doesn't come already filled with meaning. You have to create the meaning yourself. Money doesn't buy meaning; money only buys containers.

What about success? Professional success allows you to develop your capabilities in a larger world than home and hearth, and to have those capabilities affirmed by people who have no vested interest in making you feel good. That's extremely valuable information, and important to both self-esteem and having a sense of purpose

Money and success do not, all alone, add up to happiness. Most of us know that by now, even if we are still in hot pursuit. The equation is useful to work with because it reflects what a lot of people start out thinking and it's highly visual. But, it's not a "real" equation because one side doesn't really add up to the other. A more honest, if less dramatic, way to write it might be this:

MONEY, SUCCESS, THEN HAPPINESS

Both money and success have something to do with containers. Containers are anything toward which you put resources – time, money, energy – in the expectation that something will happen. A container can be a sabbatical, a consumer purchase, a job change, a change in family status, even a change in fitness level or body shape. "If I join Weight Watchers and get thinner, then I won't be so lonely."

To take a crack at applying the point of Joan's story to your own life, consider a financial commitment you've recently made or are thinking of making, in the hope that something will happen for you. Then try answering these questions:

How much money did you commit?

What container did you buy? Did you accept a promotion, adopt a baby, make a large philanthropic pledge, or sign over your house as collateral for a loan to fund your business?

What did you expect the container to do for you? Did you think it would make you happier, less lonely, more admired, more of a player?

Can you assess whether the container you've chosen can deliver what you've asked of it? For example, if you were seeking more security in your life, quitting your job and becoming a day-trader probably isn't the right container.

If you've gotten on the wrong path, do you know how to self-correct?

If you've gotten what you want, can you allow yourself to pause and feel satisfied?

If you can allow yourself to feel satisfied, can you let that satisfaction expand
into a feeling of happiness, at least for the moment? By that I mean, can
you say to yourself "I've gotten what I longed for, and right now it's
enough"?

Is All of This Always So Long-Term?

Joan's process took five years. You may be wondering whether it
always takes that long to achieve a big breakthrough. The answer is
no. Sometimes it can take less time, sometimes more, depending on
the size of the shift you're trying to make.

> The CEO of a San Francisco company has just separated from her hus-
> band of nineteen years and bought a million-dollar home in the East Bay.
> Her house overlooks the spectacular vista of the Bay Bridge and the shim-
> mering lights of the city. I asked her how it is to live there.
> "Lonely. A lot to take care of. I get home late, and the last thing I
> want to do is go over the contractor's punch list, or start making calls
> about finding a gardener, or go out and look at furniture. Having a house
> like this has been my dream for a long time; I really thought it would
> make me happier than it has. Right now it's just another burden."

This 42-year-old executive is a brilliant business strategist. She literally "sees" the direction of her fast-moving industry eighteen to
twenty-four months out, and gets herself and her company in the
right position to benefit. She's earned a solid six-figure salary for at
least ten years, and has recently made significant money on stock
options. She has a net worth of several million dollars, depending on
the day-to-day market valuation of her assets. The choice to leave the
marriage was hers. She has no children, and no plans to have them.
Gaining financial independence and being recognized professionally have long been important goals. She's achieved both. Looking at
her words without judging her choices, we can see that she hoped
buying the million-dollar home and living among other successful
people would bring happiness. So far, happiness hasn't come.

As she and I started our work together, I offered this counsel,
drawn from my work with Joan and many others: "If you want money

and success and happiness, there's something here that needs to be figured out. Just getting more of the same, that is, more money and professional recognition, won't do it. Even more important, the skills you need to figure out 'happiness' are almost the mirror opposites of the skills you've needed to build assets and a business reputation. Now you'll need to exercise flexibility instead of control, patience instead of speed, openness instead of secrecy. You'll do well to expect the messiness of clashing human values, not the simple elegance of brilliant business judgment. You'll also need to broaden your focus to allow different story threads to come into play, not just focus laser-like on where your industry is going, or whether your investments move up, down, or stay the same."

As in Joan's situation, we can see this as another example of money buying a container – the house – to hold a certain emotional expectation. The CEO hoped the vessel would come already filled, which it did not.

I can't make this point often enough. Money does a generally good job of buying containers. Money does a generally poor job of buying emotions or feelings, such as happiness, as the filling.

No more than two or three months had passed when I had another business conversation with this CEO. I remembered to ask about the house. Our talk took place shortly before the Christmas holiday, and her tone was very different.

> "I've asked my whole extended family to come and stay with me and celebrate Christmas here. It's the first time in my life that's ever happened. Always before, I was the one without children and the one my family saw as the most rootless, so I was expected to pick up and come to them for the holidays. Now I have a place, a home, and I can expect family to come to me."

What was really different? The container had been filled – not by things money can buy, but by an inner sense of meaning placed there by this thoughtful woman. An exquisite house can mean many things for a fast-track CEO: a place to entertain business associates, a setting for glitzy political fund-raisers, a choice focus for a spread in *Architectural Digest*. Instead, this CEO chose to make her home a statement of her completeness as a person, with or without husband and children, and a symbol of her being rooted, not footloose. That statement came from inside, not outside. "Inside" means that she looked more deeply into her own motivations for buying the house, and took responsibility for saying what she wanted this action to mean. "Not outside" means she wasn't looking for someone else to validate her decision. Her statement of meaning was significant in itself, regardless of how her family or anyone else invited to her home might respond.

Some of you might be shaking your heads, protesting, "Then this story really isn't about money. It's about something else, such as a woman coming into her own."

Yes, it is about money. The money bought the container. It's also about success. This CEO is not the recipient of family wealth, or a lottery winner, or a skillful white-collar crook. She made the decision years ago to take great professional risks, work enormously long hours, and sacrifice time that might have been spent on relationships in order to meet certain high standards in the business world.

To the degree that she has been able to reach inside and discover a sense of meaning in what she now finds possible, the story is also about happiness.

Might she have reached happiness without the success, the money, and the house? I don't know. Perhaps. Perhaps not. We live in a country, in an economic system, where most of us get to choose a life path. This CEO got to choose hers, and make what meaning she could of it. I suspect you have that freedom too.

Having felt a sense of happiness, is this woman done, her breakthrough complete? The answer is "not yet." Leaving her long-term marriage had an enormous emotional impact. After her family dispersed and she was once again alone, she had this to say: "It took so much emotional energy for me to leave my husband. I wonder now if I have enough life force on my own to fill up all this space. I now understand that you have to bring your own life force. It doesn't just come with buying the house."

Money stories have a long reach. They cycle back in time to pull in our families of origin. They go forward in time to test the quality of hope we are able to sustain for the future. They remind us, often in jarring ways, of the cost of continuing to grow. They evolve throughout our lifetime, picking up depth and complexity as they move through the years. Only after a person's death can we listen to his or her money story and call that part of a family money saga "done."

Taking Stock

The point of this chapter has been to give you a baseline for exploring how successful people – you included – juggle money, success, and happiness. Here are the most important elements of that baseline:

Think about money in a new way, as formative of who you are and as influential in your search for happiness.

Learn to work with the money + success = happiness equation.

Understand that the equation is deeply affected by social and cultural trends that have changed all of our lives over the past thirty years. Now, the predominant anchor for exploring the money + success = happiness equation is work, not religion or family or local community.

Remember that money buys containers. You create meaning.

As you progress through the book, I'm going to ask two things. If by chance you bought this book because you're concerned about the way someone else uses money, will you set aside that concern for the moment and focus on yourself? Quite simply, you have to work on your own experience of money before you can have integrity broaching money issues with another person. If you're in the position of depending on someone to provide for you financially, you may feel the book doesn't apply to you. It does. Each of the questions I raise is as important for people without their own direct source of income as for those who are feeling financially flush and professionally challenged. If you've never acted as if money mattered to you, you need to change that. You also need to know how you'd manage if the person now providing for you were no longer available. If you've never asked yourself how power relationships are wielded through money, you need to start. If you don't currently have the leverage you want because you know you don't have the money to walk away, how will you begin to change things?

If you've been telling yourself that despite your high-pressure life you really do keep all the balls in the air and cover all the bases, this book may challenge that belief. Becoming clear about your experience of money is absolutely fundamental to your achieving happiness. That means you need to be as honest and as non-judgmental as you can. If you grew up with a critical tape running in your head – something along the lines of "nothing I do is ever good enough" – mentally press the "pause" button and put that tape on hold. Hypercritical perfectionism will really get in your way. Also, keep in mind that taking an honest look at where you are doesn't mean instant change. If you decide later that you need to shift your behavior in some way, you get to establish the timeline and make changes when you're ready. Remembering that will help you manage any unsettled feelings that may arise.

Money is very good at buying containers in which we get to try out certain expectations. Money isn't very good at buying meaning to fill the containers – meaning has to come from inside. Learn to use money to do the things it does well, and look elsewhere for the things money does poorly or not at all.

CHAPTER TWO

Hidden Messages: Finding the Roots of Your Money Story

You've just looked at how people link money, success, and happiness. You've also taken a stab at talking more honestly about your own experience of money, at least with yourself. You've also considered an important distinction: money buys containers, and people create meaning. Now we're going to go back to your earliest experiences with money – some of which may have happened before you even had words for what you were seeing or feeling – to find out where your money story came from.

We're going to do that for two reasons. One is that your current money story didn't suddenly spring to life out of a vacuum. Your current story came from somewhere, and you need to understand where. The other reason has to do with a point made earlier: choices you have made and will make about money are deeply indicative of who you are. Your experience with money is one of the elements that shapes you. What do I mean by "shapes you"? You already know that other kinds of experiences have influenced who you are today: significant relationships, like the first time you fell in love, or significant events, such as military service or your first job. Your experience of money, now and in the past, contributes in powerful ways to the person you've become.

Explored openly, money can be a unique window into the individual we often have the hardest time seeing clearly: ourselves. Exploring the logic of money takes us "beneath the obvious" with regard to our biggest life decisions. What did you choose to do professionally, and what did income potential have to do with your choice? Where have you chosen to live, and why? What are the occupations where you wouldn't be caught dead even if you were broke? Whom do you choose as friends? Who don't you make time for in your busy life, and why? Who have you dated? Who would you marry or make a life commitment to? Will you have kids, or won't you? If you have kids, how much time do you spend with them and how much time do you spend making money? What do money or earning power have to do with making someone or something appealing to you over time?

Knowing yourself, liking your choices, and being able to take account of the needs of others, form the bedrock from which happiness can emerge. Happiness "emerges." That means happiness isn't a fleeting feeling, like the momentary high that comes from closing a big deal, or landing a key talent, or making a move that successfully captures market share. The buzz from those things fades quickly, then needs to be restimulated by yet another win. Happiness is different. Happiness is a subtle awareness that we build into our lives over time. Like a fine red wine, happiness often gets richer and more complex with age. Happiness has several elements; perhaps surprisingly, one of those is mastery. By "mastery" I mean taking charge of your life story, accepting responsibility for dealing with formative life experiences, and living with full awareness and intention in the present.

Where Hidden Messages Fit In

Taking charge of your life story isn't something that happens easily. Accepting responsibility for your early formative experiences isn't automatic; sometimes the messages contained in those early experiences are largely hidden from view. Getting yourself into the game isn't a small task; it often takes great courage, and a willingness to tolerate some anxiety while you're in the process of sorting matters out.

Consider the case of James, a successful analyst in his early 50's who came to see me about a compensation issue that was causing him great unhappiness. Although earning a low six-figure income, he felt vastly underpaid compared with his deal-making partners. As I probed further, James told me that he hadn't tried asking his partners to renegotiate the way profits were shared among them. He paused a moment, then grinned ruefully. "I guess I've never initiated a discussion of getting more money in any job I've had, even going all the way back to when I was a kid peddling ice cream out of a truck."

As James talked more about the sophisticated analyses he regularly performed, I grew puzzled. He clearly had the intelligence and verbal skill to raise the partnership issues over money. What was keeping him from putting those abilities to use on his own behalf? I asked, and he said he didn't know.

To get more data, I suggested that James complete a Money Autobiography, which is a retelling of significant life events from the perspective of money. When he returned to my office, written story in hand, he was bemused. One word had recurred repeatedly: "cheap." James' father had earned very little money when James and his brothers were young. The family had eaten cheap food, worn cheap shoes and clothes, lived in cheap neighborhoods, taken cheap transportation. Although his father later changed jobs and earned more money, James received no financial help at all during his college years; he paid his college expenses entirely on his own. Finally, when James was an adult, his father had shifted to commercial real estate and become a wealthy man.

The older man's money story had changed dramatically over time, while James' own money story had hardly changed at all. As a young boy he internalized the message – certainly never spoken – that he was only entitled to that which could be gotten cheaply. He had never tested that message with his parents, never spoken of his shame at wearing inexpensive and poorly made clothing, never mentioned his feelings of hurt and abandonment at being cut loose financially when it was time for college. He had carried a hidden message – that he wasn't worth spending money on – for all of his adulthood, and it had haunted his professional advancement.

How Hidden Messages Work

Early in life all of us, like James, are dealt certain cards. One of those is a family money story. When we're very young, we get "handed" our role in that story. The story is rarely told to us in so many words. Instead, the story is told in gestures, actions, bits and pieces of conversations overheard, in a raft of hidden messages. In one family the father may have doled out household money from his weekly paycheck; the mother secreted small amounts away so she could buy a few things without having to ask. What was the unspoken message? "Money is about control; people who earn money have more control than people who don't." What role was conveyed to the child? "See, but protect mother by not telling." In another family the mother may have been ambitious and loved working, but always referred to her earnings as "pin money" to avoid shaming the primary breadwinner, her husband. What was the unspoken message? "Money is about relationships, and about roles. Upsetting those roles can be very risky." The child's part might come across thus: "Play along with the drama by always going to Father, not Mother, for movie money, for allowance, for the dollar to save on banking day at school. Family life will remain happier that way."

The family money story always has an emotional overlay. Charmaine grew up in a family that ran a small retail store. Attitudes about money were relaxed; when the kids needed money, they asked their parents' permission and were directed to take the necessary small bills from the unlocked cash register. That relaxed approach toward money, embedded in early childhood, continued for Charmaine as she grew older. When she and her husband first opened their own retail liquor store, they made a critical buying error, stocking the shelves with $10,000 worth of Scotch wrapped in holly berries for the Christmas holiday. None sold. I asked what happened next, and Charmaine burst into peals of laughter. "I stuck the whole lot back in the storeroom, and brought it out again in the middle of the summer. We announced a Christmas in July sale, and every bottle sold."

Many new entrepreneurs suffer greatly when they make an early bad decision, even questioning whether they may have made a mistake becoming entrepreneurs at all. That was not true for Charmaine. A relaxed attitude toward money allows her the psychic room to mull over problems without undue anxiety or distress. Here, by being able to focus on solutions – "How can I turn a $10,000 error around?" – she was able to convert a poor buying decision into a good enough outcome.

Amy, on the other hand, grew up in a family where attitudes around money had to do with control, secrecy, and deception. Her father was a physician; her mother ran the home and raised the children. Amy remembers her mother relishing her prowess at the game of getting money from a man. "Oh, your father gives me an allowance but I get whatever I want." The feeling tone Amy picked up – which her mother never expressed in words – was anger. "My father loved to travel. Travel was hard for my mother because of her rheumatoid arthritis. They would drive somewhere, and he would go off and do things. When they got back to the hotel she would spend his money. She spent a lot of money. I surmise there was some payback in it. She was paying him back for going off and leaving her sitting in the car." As with Charmaine, the family's emotional overlay around money stayed with Amy into adulthood. Although a highly skilled professional, she has difficulty charging enough for her services, anxious that if she were really financially successful she would somehow be leaving her mother behind.

The truth of a family money story is often hidden beneath the actual words. The president of a manufacturing company had both a son and a daughter, the daughter the brighter of the two children by far. Both were given good educations, encouraged to have careers, and praised for their abilities. When it came time for the president to consider a succession plan, he offered the running of the business to his son, but not his daughter. When the son showed no interest, the company was sold – again without family consultation beyond the two men. The spoken story with which the children were raised was one of equality, future expectations, and opportunity. The truth of the family money story was more like this: "Running companies is for men. Women, if they work outside the home, join helping professions." The daughter, who did gain her share of the distribution but lost the opportunity to run the company, had become a social worker. A strong sense of betrayal over her father's actions interfered with her ability to find happiness in her chosen profession, and in the financial security that was now hers.

Family money stories, and the emotions they generate, typically cascade from generation to generation, becoming relatively more resolved or relatively more destructive as they barrel along. My maternal grandfather was an inventor who owned an elevator company in Manhattan; the family had a car, a radio, winter coats trimmed with fur, and summer vacations at the lake. He lost the business during the Great Depression – not because of the economic downturn, but because of his alcoholism. My mother, the fifth of ten children, remembers the good times, and also the bad. Her mother put up cheap plywood partitions in the large rooms and took in boarders. The family accepted food baskets. Those old enough left high school and did factory work to help support the others. The hidden story was not one of resourcefulness and initiative, as the facts could have supported, but one of overwhelming anxiety and shame. The drama of "having, then losing" repeated itself in my mother's adult life. At the age of 49, a few months after we had moved into a nice home in a better part of town, my father suddenly died, leaving my mother with modest insurance, three children to raise, nineteen years out of the job market, and intense anxiety about money. The anxiety, magnified by this second loss and the fear that "whatever security one has can suddenly vanish," entered a third generation and became part of my own story growing up. The anxiety about money remained with me well into adulthood, even after the level of financial security I'd reached made those feelings no longer rational.

Family money stories are hard to unearth. A kind of "surface" money talk runs rampant in our culture. We all know who makes more, Tiger Woods or the president of the United States. We all know it takes a lot of money to shop at Saks, and not a lot to purchase used knick-knacks at a flea market. We know that big donors get photographed with the senator, while small donors watch him on the evening news. We know that anyone can win the lottery just by picking the right numbers, but you have to be telegenic and smart to be invited to play the millionaire game on TV.

What counts more are the money stories we don't get to "know," at least openly, and the conversations we don't get to have. Why do we maintain such a code of silence on the deeper issues money always presents? Why is money the final unbroken taboo? In 1999, talk about explicit sexual practices became a formal part of the *Congressional Record* via the Starr investigation. In 2000, talk about religion played a significant role in the presidential election. Only money and its hidden influence remain in a verbal lockdown for most of us. The most important reasons are:

Social custom. Most of us were raised to think that asking someone directly how much an article of clothing cost, or commenting out loud on the differences in the homes of rich friends and poorer friends, is in bad taste.

Confusion about the difference between privacy and secrecy. If a stranger or casual acquaintance asked how much money you or I make, most of us probably wouldn't answer, out of a legitimate sense of privacy. If a spouse or partner asked how much we expect to earn in the upcoming year, we'd probably view withholding that number as keeping secrets and expect it to interfere with the standard of honesty agreed to in our relationship.

Gender-specific messages we've absorbed along the way, such as "Women never talk openly about money," or "Responsible men just don't get to quit their jobs in midstream and retreat to the woods to find themselves."

Pure power plays. The September 4, 2000 issue of The Industry Standard described those of us who hold tight to financial information in the workplace as exerting control. "There is no better way for entrenched interests to defend their power than to deny outsiders the ability to understand even the nature of that power." (p. 11)

Since so much about money is shrouded in silence, I call dealing with hidden money messages the equivalent of "rocket science," in the sense that the messages and their real meaning are devilishly difficult to unearth and put to good use. Simply figuring out how to make money is not rocket science. Figuring out how to get money, at least for those at the top 40% of income-earning households, has proved relatively do-able. The hard part is breaking through to our hidden money attitudes, beliefs, and understandings and figuring out how those affect our lives now. The truly satisfying work begins when we can integrate our adult values and beliefs with our current money behavior.

Can the Impact of
Hidden Messages Be Altered?

The answer is unequivocally "yes."

James wasn't disturbed or depressed, but he did need to do what I call "mental catch-up." He was acting relative to his compensation as if he were still a poor boy with a tightwad father. To resolve his career dissatisfaction, he needed to be who he is now: a well-educated, highly intelligent man with a valuable professional expertise. Once the reason for his feeling undervalued became clear – that he was subconsciously living an old, outdated story – it took James no time at all to begin renegotiation of the partnership agreement. Once he accurately saw the problem that had held him back, his integration of old and new story was completed in a matter of months.

James' story might suggest that all hidden money messages are old, stemming from early experiences and subject to quick resolution once their impact upon us is held up to the light of day. Not so; some old messages are harder to work through and take a long time and much support to resolve. And although lots of messages are old, we also deal every day with veiled money messages that are quite current.

Several years ago I was asked to consult with an energetic young project team assembled by the CEO of an old-line corporation struggling to become innovative. Assigned to the team were three senior managers acting in the role of advisors. In the moments before we first settled down to work, the three senior people were loudly exchanging war stories about a seemingly unrelated topic: the horrors of frequent business travel. They especially bemoaned the stress of being booked from time to time on small commuter prop-planes instead of on full-size jets.

"Besides the noise and lousy service," one manager said, shaking his head in disgust," there's a real difference in how those guys get paid compared to the pilots of real planes. We must be crazy. How can we put our lives in the hands of guys who only make $60,000 a year?"

The man's spoken words conveyed one message: people who make as little as $60,000 a year can't be trusted to fly planes safely. There was also a veiled underlay, directed consciously or unconsciously toward the younger and less highly paid members of the team. To my ears the veiled message went something like this: "We senior guys make a lot more than $60,000 a year. People who make more money can be trusted with important decisions; people who don't, can't. When it comes time to make big decisions here, plan on looking to us." The veiled message might even have stated this: "Anyone who really has what it takes to make such huge decisions would be where we are financially, not where you are."

The team was clearly getting two messages. One was the literal, spoken mandate from the CEO: "Solve this problem. I'm giving you the help of three of my best senior people." The other message was harder to detect, and came from the senior managers themselves. "Don't even think of strutting your stuff over our heads. We get the big salaries to be the decision makers in this company, not you."

The result was, as one might expect, immobility rather than innovation. In this case, leaving the message veiled, instead of testing it openly, stood as an effective block to any real change.

Why Not Just Suck
It Up and Move On?

Why should anyone bother with all this "hidden message" stuff? James led a busy life; he was not by nature especially reflective, and he came to me to solve a current problem, not to reexamine a childhood whose effects were long ago ingrained. The innovation team was under the gun in a competitive marketplace; they sought me out to help accelerate the team's progress, not to slow them down with what might have seemed like cross-functional navel-gazing. There's a strong penchant in our culture for sucking it up and moving forward, especially where conflict or anger are involved. That's the mantra of new technology workers, who often maintain they have "no time for reflection." What difference can old events, long-forgotten and buried, really make? Why should we train our ears in current time to listen for the "message beneath the message," when figuring out what people say in the first place takes more time than we have?

My sense of the answer to these questions comes from years of thoughtful experience with clients. From that perspective, I know of several reasons why unearthing old messages sooner rather than later really matters.

Being sophisticated about money in one part of your life and naive about money in another is downright dangerous. The forty-year-old president of a successful corporate communications company drives a $10 million operating budget. She and I were discussing the upcoming negotiation of her contract when she casually mentioned her year-end bonus. "One of these times I need to take all this money and work with a financial advisor. I don't even really know what a stock is." On the professional side, this very bright woman knows very well what money does – how money drives strategy, how delivering on profitability at the local level wins you a seat at the corporate strategy table, how failing at profitability leaves you out of the conversation and out in the cold. Yet on the personal side she doesn't really know what a stock is. The gap is dangerous. If you're sophisticated about money in one setting, people can easily assume you're sophisticated about money, period. You can get in way over your head way too quickly. You can be ashamed to admit what you don't know, afraid to ask for help because a person at your level would sound like a fool. It's a little like the remnants of Spanish I retain from my Peace Corps days in rural Panama. What I can still say, I say with appropriate fluency and accent. Native Spanish speakers, thinking I'm still bilingual, barrage me with lengthy responses. I wind up grinning glassy-eyed at them while trying to figure out how to say gracefully, in English, "I lost you on the third sentence and have no idea what you just said. I hate to ask you to repeat the whole thing in English, but would you please?" In this case, my client's determination to have nothing to do

with money on the personal side wasn't about lack of skill or expo-
sure. Rather, it had to do with growing up in a family business that
was too often touch-and-go and that continually seemed to suck her
parents' emotional energy dry. We had to delve into that, painful
though it was, before she could take concrete steps toward gaining
control of her personal financial life.

*If you remain oblivious to the hidden messages that drive your career
choices, you can wind up deeply unhappy and in a financial bind.* Consider
the case of a pediatric oncologist I know. Becoming an oncologist
takes a very long time and costs a fortune in loans. There's college,
medical school, internship, residency, then further specialty training.
You probably have to borrow more money to establish a practice. You
might well be almost 40 before you really begin to reverse the accu-
mulation of debt and start to get on your financial feet. You might
well have a wife who doesn't work outside the home and small children; your wife is relieved that the lean years are over, and that you
can finally enjoy life as a family. She wants to move to a bigger home
in a neighborhood with better schools. This is the moment you lift
your nose from the grindstone, suspect you've been living out someone else's dream, not your own, and realize that you hate the work.
Since this young doctor had been in fact practicing oncology for
many years prior to our conversation, I doubt this was his first inkling
that that medicine was not for him. It was simply the first inking he
allowed to break through his very determined forward trajectory. So
anxiety-provoking was the appearance of this hidden underlay, so dis-
orienting were the words "I don't think I want to be a pediatric oncologist any more," that this brilliant and confident man spoke in mere
whispers. It took a long time before he could even begin to believe
that a way might emerge for his next 25 years of professional life to
be different.

*If painful earlier experiences have been submerged but never resolved, you
risk unintentionally repeating them.* A very ambitious corporate executive regularly worked twelve- to fourteen-hour weekdays, part of both
weekend days, and traveled often. He earned nearly $300,000 a year
plus bonus, was frugal and exceedingly driven about building a financial cushion for his wife and small children. He was successful at that,

although his children saw him very little. He came to me because, although good at his career, he felt unsettled and unhappy and wondered about changing jobs. By way of background, I asked him to tell me what his father did for a living, since parents are often primary role models for our understanding of "work." His jaw tightened. "My father died when I was very young." He and his mother were not left destitute, but money was very tight. As an adult, he was adamant about controlling for that risk in the lives of his own children by making sure they had a big financial cushion. I pointed out gently that he and his children shared an experience that was perhaps not yet visible to him: both had fathers not much present in their lives. I asked if some balancing might be possible between his need to make his family financially secure and his children's need to know him. That quest took our work with "I feel unsettled and unhappy about my job" in a very different direction from "Is there another company, another twist on these skills that I've developed, that might be more satisfying for me?"

Here's the point of these stories: If you want to use money as a window into who you really are, if you want to use money to lead you into the complex terrain of happiness and professional fulfillment, you need to look deeper. Hidden messages, kept in play by the powerful unconscious, count much more than you've allowed yourself to believe. Said another way: you have to pick up the cards you were dealt at birth in order to get really into the game. You're unnecessarily hamstrung if you go through life leaving your formative experiences on the table and pass up the chance to see how their messages continue to influence you.

What Good Will It Do to Go Down This Road?

Old hidden messages about money really count. So do current, veiled messages that happen because people are given the sense that talking openly about money and the influence it conveys is bad. What are the benefits that can come when you expose such messages to the light of day?

If you can bring old messages current and make them conscious – the process I call "mental catch-up" – you have choices. You might find the hidden message more positive than the words you remember actually being spoken. In that case, you can keep attitudes and beliefs you find valuable, and perhaps make them even more powerful in your current life. You can tinker with the messages, keeping some aspects intact and changing others, or you can discard messages that hold you back and no longer serve any constructive purpose. James did the last; he discarded the message that he wasn't worth much. By opening his partnership agreement to renegotiation, he wrote a new story along these lines: "I have a valuable skill, and I choose to be in a work setting where I can be paid what that skill is worth." He was happy with the professional outcome, which meant a job change, and happy with himself.

If you can bring current veiled messages out into the open, you can deal with real issues and make changes that will stick. The innovation team's problem wasn't a lack of ability to see and deliver on cutting-edge products. The problem was a culture clash between old and new ways of thinking. The CEO, having failed thus far to drive his desire for change down through the phalanx of his senior managers, had consciously or unconsciously elected to go about it the other way. He set up a team of bright and ambitious young Turks, threw three senior people into the mix, and said, "Go to it." For some time the team had been spinning their wheels making modifications to the product. They hoped making the product better, simpler, more profitable, more easily integrated with the rest of the product mix, would overcome resistance to their efforts. Those modifications were important, but they weren't the real issue. The real issue was cutting a deal between the people who had made the company successful in the past but felt left behind, and those who were going to make the company move faster, act smarter, and learn to take bigger risks. With such an understanding, both groups could pull together in the future. Not surprisingly, the tool to get at the real issue was money, and the opening was created by the banter of the senior managers themselves. For this organization to change, the deeply held belief that "The guys who get paid most always get to be at the front of the charge" had to shift. The new story line had to become "The people who think smartest about any given challenge get to run with it, and it's everyone else's role to kick away barriers and find resources to support the run."

What truths do these stories point out? You have to make old money messages current. It's smart to make veiled money messages open. You can use money as a tool to gain entry into hard conversations, so you can get at the real issues. Most importantly, you need to integrate money into who you are now, so you can actively test out what money can do. You'll gain a sense of mastery, and be happier that way.

Adding This New Element to Your Money Story

If what's been said so far has given you a slight sense of discomfort, as in "I can see how this might apply to me, but I have no idea how to uncover hidden messages and incorporate them into my story," here are some suggestions:

Pay attention to what I call "tics" in your experience. "Tics" are momentary incongruities or inconsistencies – things that stand out as not making sense. Tics in your experience mean something. For the president of a company to manage an operating budget with confidence, but be oblivious to basic tools of personal financial security, is incongruous. One could plead lack of time, lack of interest in the personal side of money, or lack of a "mind for investing." The real culprits, I'd say, are old money messages unconsciously creating havoc.

When you suspect a hidden money message is on board, look into it. In the Appendix to the book there is a sample Money Autobiography, which you can use if you like to write and if that process would be useful to you. If not, here's the short version to jump-start your thinking. You don't have to write; just let your mind wander over the questions, and see what emerges.

> *"When's the first time you remember having money? Who gave it to you? How free were you to decide what to do with the money? What did you do with it?"*

"When's the first time you remember earning money? How did you earn it? What did you do with it?

"Have you ever seen money used to create goodness? What has carried over from that experience to your life now?

"Have you ever seen money used in a way that hurt other people? What did you take away from that?"

"When you face money decisions, how do you usually feel? Elated? Challenged? Sad? Afraid? Anxious? Other? Do you know why?"

"What's the hardest experience you've ever had in which money played some part, either openly or covertly? What happened? What was the fallout from that experience for you? What have you carried forward in terms of the way you act with money now?"

As you begin delving into old messages, don't stop with the literal role money played. Remember that money also "stands in" for other things, like a behavior that hurt us or a person who disappointed us. That's the symbolic meaning of money. If you're often mad or resentful at money, try considering whether it's really the money, or whether you might be upset with someone who stood behind the money. Be prepared for that realization to cause you some anxiety. You can be mad at money, and it will never talk back or challenge your perceptions of what happened. If you're mad at someone, especially someone who matters in your life, resolving that will be much more complicated. Following a workshop session I once conducted, a participant came up to relate this story. He said he'd always had a great disdain for money, and as a result never really earned much from his professional practice. He hadn't a clue why until I asked the group "Have you ever seen money used in a way that hurt other people?" The question hit him like an electric shock. When he was very young his father had abandoned the family, leaving him and his mother in desperate financial straits. His paternal grandfather was wealthy, and his mother used to send him to his grandfather to ask for money, which he hated. I asked gently if he thought money was the real object of his disdain. Now able to look at past experience through the eyes of an adult, he saw that his feelings were more likely centered on his father's abandonment and on his having to shoulder a responsibility for getting money from his grandfather at far too young an age. I asked if he had a support system to help him deal with these painful issues once he returned home. He said he did, and promised to seek it out.

Sometimes hidden messages can be funny, whimsical, or just outdated. In that case they may be influencing our behavior, but without too much emotional punch. At other times, old messages made conscious can be devastating. If that happens, seek out the appropriate support. People sometimes ask me "When should I see someone like you, and when should I see a therapist about my money issues?" There are two instances, in my view, in which good therapeutic intervention is essential. One is when money leads you to deeply painful psychological issues – abandonment, loss, fear of intimacy – and you become overwhelmed with anxiety and depression. The other is when you really "get" what's going on with you and money and still can't change your behavior. That's a signal that more is involved than what I term "mental catch-up," and you may need a deeper intervention to help you get over being stuck.

Old messages often involve experiences with other family members. If you decide to seek them out and reality-test your own perceptions, your motivation in doing so makes all the difference. Time goes forward, not backward. What happened to you in the past is set in stone. It's done, and can't be changed. You may get more data by opening up a conversation, you may be able to work a process of forgiveness, but you can't change whatever happened to you in the past. Kate Schroeder-Bruce, a psychiatric nurse practitioner and a therapist in private practice, says this of opening old money messages with other family members:

> The important thing in opening up this conversation is the person's intention. What is the expectation? What is the hope? Many of the things that will be discussed cannot be changed. They've happened. They're over. They're in the past. To want this to be about something the person didn't get at a younger age is risky. The real point of the conversation is the power of the narrative story. It's very hard to just listen to the story, listen to what the other person is saying about his or her experience. It's especially hard in families, because the experiences are intertwined.

Even if you can't change the past, you can create healing going forward. If you weren't given the appropriate tools and experiences to learn about money when you were a child, you can give those things to your children, your nieces and nephews, your students, the people you supervise. If you were denied as a child and now have the wherewithal, you can create opportunities for other children. If money in your family was a source of great anxiety, you can intentionally make it simpler and less emotion-ridden now. Often, when I speak with people who are intimidated by the very idea of investing, I say this: "Look, the stock market does three things. It goes up, down, or stays the same. No one, not even the best of professional money managers, knows what any given investment will do on any given day. No one picks winners all the time. If you do choose to become active in growing your money, you'll make mistakes and lose money here and there. That doesn't matter. What matters is that you come to view this as a learning process at which you'll get better over time."

When you decide to use money as a tool to get at the real issues, be sure you have adequate conflict resolution skills. In the first place, being more honest and direct about money is counterculture. For one of the young Turks to have turned to a senior manager and asked "Does your comment about not trusting people who only make $60,000 a year have anything to do with us?" would have broken an unwritten taboo within that organization. In the second place, although you may feel that you've dealt pretty well with your own money issues, you can't make assumptions about anyone else. Your directness may hit some painful hot buttons for others. Finally there's a shocking lack of understanding, even among otherwise well-educated people, about basic business models and concepts like "profitability." At another workshop gathering, a business owner shared the experience of having opened his books to his employees so that everyone could understand what they were working toward in terms of growth and profitability. Instead of being motivated, the employees were furious they weren't being paid more and that he was taking so much out of the business. That points to two things: a need for much greater education about how profitability works in a business setting, and an honest examination on the part of the business owner about how much he takes out versus what he shares with his employees.

Whether you're delving into old hidden messages or focusing on the "dual layer" of money talk in our present culture, the key point is linking both to your life now, and seeing what needs to change. Doing the hidden message part of money isn't about navel-gazing, it's about mastery. It's valuable for the oncologist to realize he'd been living someone else's professional dream for twenty years, but only half the point. Finding happiness and professional fulfillment now means making decisions about the next twenty-five years of his life. Sometimes, when people are faced with a scenario like this, they're tempted to polarize, to make it all about money, or not about money at all but about finding your heart. Well, it's about both. Surely the oncologist has a very, very big financial problem as he considers a career change, and that can't be minimized. The problem affects not only him, but also his wife and children. They may have to accept a more modest lifestyle even longer than his wife had hoped. She may have to reevaluate her decision not to work outside the home. He may at least reconsider whether there's an area of medicine – teaching, perhaps – that would allow him to make use of his long training but not require him to treat desperately ill children. Or, he may combine his latent interest in business with his knowledge of a medical specialty to form a new venture focused on a medical product or service. At the same time, the dilemma he faces is about finding his heart. It would be tragic, in my view, for him to spend another twenty-five years doing work that's well-paid and prestigious, but that he simply doesn't like. What we're talking about here is "integration." Money and prestige are big issues in life; so is our heart's desire. They all count together.

The Payback for Facing Hard Truths

I've made the case for understanding the "silent subtext" of your money story by uncloaking hidden or veiled money messages. Refuse to be content with having these messages act on you in ways you don't really grasp or pay attention to. Instead, take responsibility for making beliefs and attitudes about money current, and making them your own. Sound like a lot of effort? Here's what you're going to gain, probably sooner rather than later:

You can move from being acted upon by hidden yet powerful messages to being in charge of your choices and your destiny.

You can actually change patterns that may still be destructive in your life, with the added possibility of influencing family members and work colleagues in positive ways.

You'll be able to have more intelligent conversation about the use of money in the global arena where you hope to make your mark.

According to a World Bank study released in 2000, 2.8 billion of the world's people – almost half the planet's population – survive on a daily income of less than $2. Part of your current level of success has to do with an accident of birth; you were born here, not there. Figuring out how to connect "there" with "here" has something to do with making a lasting footprint on the larger world, not just your tiny corner, before you can consider yourself fulfilled.

Dealing with money messages may sound matter-of-fact, as if you notice these "tics" in experience, figure them out, and then make the necessary behavioral changes. The problem gets solved, and the benefits are in the bag. In fact, it doesn't usually work that way. Hidden or veiled money messages are often intertwined with high emotional drama. That makes the process far more dynamic. The benefits don't come cheaply or with a casual effort. They take work. If you want money to serve as a window into happiness and professional fulfillment, you have to purposely see money in that larger role.

It's not unusual for money messages to be intertwined with emotions that are, or seem, life and death. Laurie is in her mid-40's, a successful entrepreneur in the field of strategic e-business consulting. About thirty years ago, when she was 17, her parents were in a major car accident. Her mother was dead on arrival at the emergency ward, although doctors were able to revive her. The injured woman's life hung by a thread for the next two days. Brought to the hospital by her father, Laurie found her mother semi-conscious, in intensive care, and with tubes coming out of every possible part of her body. Laurie was sure her mother was dying. Laurie went to the head of her mother's bed, held her mother's hand, whispered "it's me," and told her mother she was glad to see her.

Realizing Laurie was in the room, her mother began to speak in an agitated fashion. As Laurie remembers the moment, her mother said, "Laurie, you need to go home and pay the bills. They're due on the 14th and they have to be sent in, or we'll lose our credit and lose the business." Laurie assured her mother that she would do her best and that her mother shouldn't worry.

That' s what I call a "tic in experience" – the deathbed message is not, "I love you," but, "go home and pay the bills." I find it jarring even to write.

Laurie recalls the message she heard as a 17-year-old and carried into adulthood.

There really isn't time in life for grieving/dying when there are bills to pay. I was devastated by the fact that my mother might die. However, I had to spend the time right after her accident trying to keep the family business afloat. Responsibilities come first. Certainly my dad helped. However, he was no more knowledgeable than I was since my mother had always done the administration of the business. Running your own business is an all-or-nothing endeavor. You are "it" as far as resources are concerned. When you get injured, or die, or become incapacitated, the business gets into big trouble and can die too. In the end we got the bills paid on time and eventually my mother recovered, even though it was a year long ordeal, including all the psychological trauma she went through.

People who have an early encounter with life's fragile side – because someone they love dies, or might die – have the potential to see the world with different eyes. They realize, if they let the message penetrate, that we all live "on the edge" all the time. Anyone's life can change in the most fleeting of moments. Most of us don't think about that, because we don't have occasion to. Laurie did have occasion to think about it, at least in the moment when she first approached her mother's bedside. That "life can't be taken for granted" is a very clarifying piece of wisdom for a 17-year-old, or for anyone, when it comes to deciding what's really important. It's especially valuable for the type-A personalities with their "just until . . ." mentality; the belief that 80-hour work weeks are fine just until the next big deal closes, or the next new person comes on board, or the latest profitability target is reached.

Such wisdom can be a little obscure for a 17-year-old, especially in the high emotional drama of the moment and when the real point seems so counter to Laurie's mother's actual words. The real message can fall below our psychological radar, right along with the trauma of the event. Here's a case where the hidden message is more valuable than the spoken words, and well worth going back to uncover.

Sometimes it takes an intervening experience to make us want to go back. Experiences, and the messages they impart, often cascade from one generation to the next, gaining intensity as they barrel along. Laurie and her husband have a daughter in her early teens who lives with a chronic and potentially fatal genetic illness. Medications and treatments exist to improve quality of life and enhance life span, but there is as yet no cure. Once again, life's fragile side comes calling, albeit with the roles reversed. Laurie is now the mother; it's the daughter, energetic and winsome in her eagerness for life, who dances on the edge. Laurie is also in the second year of building her national consulting practice, and the time demands on her are great. The prevailing message, the one she got from her mother, was this: "Responsibilities come first. Running a business is an all-or-nothing endeavor."

I didn't know Laurie when she was 17, nor have I ever met her mother. I would guess the mother is a no-nonsense woman, hard working, not much given to displays of emotion. Like most of us, I imagine she might have been terrified in the moment of her near-death. The message I suspect was hidden beneath her actual words might have been something like this:

> I just almost died. I'm still afraid I might die. I don't know how to tell you how much I love you, how much I depend on you and trust you. I'm not used to putting feelings like that into words. You're the one I look to if I can't be there to do what needs to be done for the family. I look to you more than I look to your father, more than I look to any of your siblings. I'd give anything not to have to ask you to shoulder

this responsibility. I can't even get the words out. So I'm going to talk about the bills, and trust you to understand what I really mean.

The hidden message, in this case, is a good one. The hidden message contains the real wisdom of the moment, wisdom that should be kept intact and made even more of a factor in Laurie's daily life. The real wisdom is not "business comes first; I'd rather you go pay the bills than be with me as I struggle not to die." The real wisdom is "life is fragile. We shouldn't wait until crisis moments, when words may fall short, to tell each other how much love and trust there is between us. We shouldn't wait until crisis moments to let it be seen that we care."

That message gives Laurie a balancing point between the demands of the business she's creating and the needs of her daughter, her son, her husband, and her extended family. The growth point for her, the behavioral shift, is to practice putting into words the emotions her mother modeled pushing away.

Healing takes place by going forward, not backward. Laurie has a powerful opportunity to master the fear conveyed by her mother: fear of loving too deeply what we know we can lose. Laurie also has the opportunity to take charge of her goals for the business. With the real message in mind, Laurie can set her own "How much is enough?" standard for assessing professional success, instead of simply accepting "Business always comes first."

You've now been able to explore the roots of money stories. Hopefully, that has allowed you to dig more deeply into your own life. Understanding how tenacious early experience can be is crucially important to your decisions about money now and in the future.

With "old" and "current" aspects of your money story fully underway, the next chapter will introduce your goal for the future: integration, or making money an ordinary part of life. Remember that hidden money messages work on you; left hidden, they rarely work for you. Make money both "more" and "less"; make it more ordinary as conversation, and less overbearing as an influence.

Take charge of what money can do, and write yourself a new and more powerful story. Know that high drama is often attached to money. Don't try to make its link with happiness logical and emotionless, which it almost never is.

Chapter Three

The Promise of "Integration": Making Money Ordinary

"Make money ordinary" means making money something we learn about in the course of daily life, just as we learn about other things: fly fishing, or how to get from New York to Luang Prabang, or how to be good parents. By that standard, we should become more skilled and more at ease with money as we age. Making money ordinary also means accepting the power money always conveys, and learning to use that power in ways that reflect our hope for the future.

What do we need to know to make money ordinary? We need to know that money has its own story, and that story is a powerful thread in each of our lives, whether acknowledged or not. We need to know that not talking openly about experiences with money hampers our ability to learn. We need to know that we began to accumulate images and feelings about money at a very young age, perhaps before we even had words to put to those images. We learned first by watching our mothers or primary caregivers. Our fathers may have been the ones who earned money, but as very young children we mostly saw them go out of the house, and come back. It was our mothers whom we saw doing things like hiding their "pin money" in the unused sugar bowl, and then tucking the bowl away in the back of the cupboard. As we got a bit older, we watched both parents. Finally, as we got out into the world, we expanded our financial horizons by watching and listening to an ever-widening circle of people.

We need to know that the impact of old experiences, if not addressed and modified by adult insight, can accelerate in strength as time passes and have a profound impact on our current choices. We need to know that money, just like any power source, carries a jolt – including an emotional impact – and needs to be handled with care. We need to know that the power money provides can be used for good or for ill, and that we're accountable for that use.

In this chapter we're going to talk about four stages of relating to money: denial, anxiety, exploration, and integration. Looking at how you relate to money now will draw your attention back from the past, from the history of your money story, and firmly ground you in current time. That's an essential step as you prepare to tackle money's hardest questions. Remember that in order to feel differently about your money, you have to act differently from now on. Simply understanding how you got here isn't enough.

What's a "Money Stage"?

Sixty-year-old Eric, a retired educator and artist, became a millionaire the old-fashioned way, through lifelong habits of frugality and careful investing. His net worth got a low six-figure boost from the estate of his mother, a single parent and bank clerk who never earned much in salary but who saved rigorously and had a secret passion for stocks. Upon her death a stockbroker called Eric with mind-boggling news: his mother's hot hand had yielded a robust portfolio that he soon received as an inheritance.

Eric is a frequent and curious traveler. Planning a repeat trip to Turkey, he faced a lengthy journey between two cities on his itinerary. A plane ticket cost $82 and would cover the distance in one hour. A bus ride over difficult and not especially scenic terrain cost just $15, but would consume 12 precious hours.

"How," I asked him, "do you plan to make that part of your trip?"
He glared at me. "By bus, of course."

I shook my head. "Eric, you're a millionaire. Take the plane."

What would you call continuing to live as if buying an $82 plane ticket is a prohibitive expense, even though you're a millionaire? I call it "denial." Eric grew up in a home where ends never did quite meet, and where it was a big event to scrape together a few coins to take the bus downtown for Saturday afternoon at the movies or at Woolworth's. Continuing to live that way suggests that Eric feels tentative, undeserving, somehow like an imposter in relation to his assets.

Denial can take other forms, like distancing from one's ambitions. The young management team of a technology company headed toward an IPO called to see if I would work with them on leadership issues and business strategy. I asked them to tell me about their company. "The first thing we want you to know," the CEO replied forcefully, "is that this isn't about money. It's about shaping the global technology story."

"Hmm," I responded skeptically. "I don't think so. You're driving a for-profit company toward an IPO, not building a network of soup kitchens. If you're successful with your business goal and complete the IPO, you're all going to make a lot of money. What makes that so hard to say?"

Examples of denial include holding one's assets at arms' length, living as if money is not really part of the picture, and lacking curiosity about the powerful role money plays in your life. Denial interferes with achieving happiness, in the sense that if you can't "see" what you have or what you're trying to get, it's hard to enjoy where you are or celebrate what you achieve.

"Denial," and the three other stages of "anxiety," "exploration," and "integration," are rough constructs. They aren't fixed in the sense that everyone must experience each stage. They aren't linear in the sense that people begin with one stage, finish with it, and then move on to another. Rather, people move in and out of the four stages with the ebb and flow of life. Someone who feels quite integrated about his or her money, values, and behavior can be flung into a state of high anxiety at the onset of a new financial obligation, such as starting a business or adding a baby to the family. Someone who has long been in denial can, step by step, begin to find some enjoyment in exploring what money can do. Someone who feels disproportionately anxious about money can often grow calmer with the experience of small steps successfully taken.

"Anxiety" can have a number of meanings in the context of a money story. For people of modest income, anxiety can be a well-grounded fear of not having enough money to pay the bills. Anxiety can also be the result of a radical change in income, as with an older woman whose cash flow fell from $400,000 a year to $60,000 when her husband's death triggered a shift in the distribution of certain assets. Anxiety can also reflect a fear of losing one's money, then losing control of one's life. When people truly don't have the money to make ends meet, they worry quite legitimately about paying bills and keeping a roof over their heads. They usually don't suffer from fears about losing their money, because they don't have money to lose. It's when people have money that they begin to fear the consequences of losing it. Periodically, during those times when the stock market dips, Eric calls me instead of his financial planner. His question is always the same. "Am I still?" What he means is, "Am I still safe, or do I need to start worrying about being old and destitute?"

Both men and women can fear outliving their assets and losing control of their lives. For women, this fear even has a specific name: it's commonly called the "bag lady fantasy." This fantasy seems to occur regardless of a woman's level of education, age, professional status, or income. Try asking any group of women you associate with – your book club, investment group, or corporate network – if they've ever worried about being bag ladies or known anyone else who did. I guarantee that several hands will go up.

Anxiety can be a very difficult and immobilizing experience. People in this stage may obsessively read the market news or watch CNBC. They make very few moves, because they fear anything they do will make their financial situation worse. As Eric began to move out of denial and accept the reality of his money, he began to experience periods of anxiety. I strongly suggested that he look at his portfolio as a long-term asset, review his monthly statements, meet with his financial advisor for a twice-yearly review, and then simply stop watching day-to-day market fluctuations.

In extreme cases, people who feel overwhelming anxiety about their money may refuse to deal with it at all. One woman in her mid-50's, whose ascetic lifestyle reflected deeply held beliefs in social justice, received a whopping inheritance on the death of her grandmother. When the woman first came to see me, she had been stuffing financial statements in a drawer and largely ignoring them, despite the desperate pleas of the broker trying to manage the account and her tax advisor. She simply couldn't get her arms around being a wealthy woman. I asked if she could give me a visual image to describe what she was experiencing. After thinking for several moments, she did.

> I feel as if I woke up one morning and a huge, out of-control plant had appeared in my garden. I don't know what the plant is, much less how to take care of it. It's too overgrown and wild to even see a spot where I might begin cutting it back. I didn't ask for it to be there. It's taking up all the sunlight, and hurting the other plants. I don't know what to do with it, so I don't do anything at all. Soon I don't even go out into the garden any more.

Her image helped me understand the overpowering nature of her good fortune. I tried to pick a small step, asking if simply gathering up the buried financial statements and bringing them in might be a place to start. She replied, "No. It would make me too anxious to do that right away." We started, instead, talking about her grandmother.

The third stage, "exploration," occurs when people really begin to experiment with what money can do and what satisfaction it can bring. This can be a stage where people make lots of expensive consumer purchases. A fascination with the buying power of money can last a long time, or not. As one weary traveler just returned from a top-of-the-line African safari remarked, "After all, how many safaris like this do you want in a lifetime?" "Exploration" can also be a stage in which people experiment with the creative power of money. A successful entrepreneur rented space for her business in an urban city center with poorly funded and low-performing schools. Liking hands-on involvement, she chose to give back to the neighborhood by adopting a classroom in the nearest school. She visited, assessed the need for supplies and equipment, and simply went out and bought things. Along came science equipment, arts and crafts supplies, and books for the quiet reading corner. The kids benefited, the teacher enjoyed a huge affirmation of her attempts to teach more creatively, and the entrepreneur got what she wanted: fast action, no bureaucracy, and visible results.

There's a really positive personal side to the exploration stage: it's the point at which people are more likely to begin to actively manage their assets, either alone or with financial advisors. It can be the first time, literally, that people put "hands on" the money.

Integration, the final stage, is the ultimate goal of making money ordinary. People who are committed to integrating money into the rest of their lives make a daily practice of paying attention to the deeper side of financial decisions, talking openly about money and what can be learned from it, and then working hard to align their behavior with their beliefs and values. Integration should always be viewed as a work in progress, not a done deal. Learning new things about the power of money happens until the day we die.

Practicing Integration

Paul, age 57, and Anita, age 55, are hard workers and always have been. They've worked for over forty years to get where they are now, which is degree of financial independence that exceeds what either grew up with.

They think they have more money than their parents did. They really don't know what Paul's father is worth, nor did Paul know his father's income or net worth at any point while growing up. He knows that his father managed a law office, was a son of the Great Depression and therefore eternally frugal, and that his parents' social circle included people who had big houses and cars, took trips, and did a lot of entertaining. Paul and Anita have a better grasp of Anita's parents' current finances, since Paul now informally advises them on investments. Anita did know money was tight when she was growing up, although specific numbers were not used. When she was four, her father, a skilled meat cutter, fell ill and was never able to work again. Her mother, a registered nurse, became the family provider, first working in a doctor's office, and then gaining the academic credentials to become a school nurse teacher. After a falling out with the grandmother who came to live with them and help, Anita's father took over household roles: cooking, cleaning, gardening. "Enough money" was hard to come by. Her parents made all financial decisions together, weighing expenditures with great care. Anita recalls one time when the decision process went badly awry: the purchase of her sister's senior prom dress. Her parents had talked about the dress and agreed on an amount in the range of $30–35. Anita, her sister, her mother, and her aunt set out to shop. They found a prom dress in the agreed-on price range and bought it. For some reason – perhaps, Anita thinks, "just to rile my father up" – the mother and aunt coached the sister to say the dress had cost $50. Her father was enraged, and it was "the last he talked to my mother for three days. I don't think she understood to what extent that would upset him."

Between themselves and with me, Paul and Anita talk quite openly about their finances. Their combined income, according to Paul, is in the "low $200,000's" with each earning about the same, and they have assets of "a couple million." Paul manages a group of project managers and consultants who work all over the country. Anita is a senior consultant in instructional design. She voluntarily gave up supervising other employees so that she and Paul can spend six months a year working remotely from their second home in a warmer climate. For Paul, that was an easy negotiation, since the people who report to him are geographically dispersed anyway. For Anita, the negotiation meant firmly pushing the envelope with her employer, who was not accustomed to employees being out of the office for six months at a time. Her job does demand frequent travel, which she does willingly if not enthusiastically.

Integration is a work in progress, never a done deal. Integration doesn't mean being without issues or financial tensions, being entirely finished with old hidden messages, or necessarily liking everything about how you fill the containers in your life with meaning. Integration means making money an ordinary part of life, no more or less powerful than any other story thread. Integration means talking about and learning from experience. Integration means using financial power to implement one's deepest values and beliefs – in the case of this twenty-five-year marriage, with shared values and beliefs.

Money is an ordinary part of Paul and Anita's life, not a mystery or a secret. They work with a financial advisor and pay attention to their portfolios. Paul watches CNBC, and tracks his accounts on a weekly basis. Paul and Anita respect each other's earning capacity. They talk over and agree on large purchases, like a new car or the remodeling of their second home. They do learn from experience. Paul had a natural curiosity about money from a young age. He began working when he was 13, unloading trucks for 75 cents an hour. When he was around 14 he asked his father to help him set up a bro-kerage account, even though his father had never himself invested. Later, when Paul graduated from college and began working, his first boss took him aside. The older man advised him to save part of his salary every week, and to put his annual bonus in the savings plan instead of spending it, saying, "When it comes time to retire, you'll thank me." When Paul was promoted to a level where he began to be paid every four weeks, one of the more senior managers explained to him "This works better, once you get used to it. You'll have a larger pool of capital to work with, and it will be easier to budget and save." Paul found that to be true, and learned what having a pool of money at one time can mean in terms of having more flexibility in financial choices.

Anita came out of her childhood experience with money carry-ing a strong message that her mother "hammered into my sister and me." The girls were told: "You will go to college and learn to do some-thing – not study English and history, but come out of college with a trade so that you can support your family like me." Anita's chosen field was computers and data processing. On graduating college in the mid-1960s she and a girlfriend had "the highest offers of anyone." She worked in an organization of all men, some of whom she exceeded in salary. Unlike Paul, she did not get mentoring and advice about money from the men she worked for. In contrast to the tight control over money she had seen growing up, she became a spend-thrift, buying all the best clothes and using her weekly salary to have a good time. She learned about money after she met Paul. Looking back, she reflects on that turning point. "If I hadn't met Paul, I don't know if I would have turned it around." She has turned it around, and now has her own pool of capital that reflects her earnings and investments.

Anita and Paul have done some exploration with money. They purchased their second home, and undertook a major renovation to make it just the way they want it. They have started trust funds for their grandchildren. They continue to be "hands-on" with their accounts and to learn. Paul is now mastering covered call writing, an options strategy that allows him to reduce the downside risk of certain of his stock holdings. Anita continues to be actively engaged with their financial advisor, mastering the financial concepts that are driving the growth of her portfolio.

In short, they integrate money into their daily life. They talk about it. Paul worries about market downturns, about trying to balance a "stop and smell the roses" philosophy with the sense that if he stops working, things might be a lot harder in old age. He saw his own mother grow ill and need expensive care. He also has the example of Anita's mother, who now lives in an eldercare facility where, although well taken care of, she "is at the mercy of others." Anita worries about not being able to enjoy their money. She is still less frugal than Paul, and worries about spending even the money that she earns herself out of fear Paul will disapprove. Although laughing as she speaks, she says, "Paul makes me worry. I wouldn't just go buy a car. I wouldn't dare. I'd want to be able to come home that night."

I ask if Paul has responded badly to things she has bought. She went back to an incident much earlier in their marriage, where she had jokingly said to Paul, "If you just buy me this, I'll be happy." Anita and Paul's marriage is a second one for Paul. Unfortunately, Anita's comment replicated a constant refrain of his first wife, and he did become angry. I asked if he had become angry since that time. Anita thought for a moment, and then responded this way: "You remember the story of the prom dress that we talked about earlier? My Dad didn't talk to us for three days. I think I remember that huge reaction from my Dad, and lay a lot of it on Paul."

Old, unresolved messages linger just below the surface in our lives, gathering steam as they barrel through time, waiting to be activated again by a similar event: in this case, a joking statement that struck a nerve and went awry.

What Can You Learn from This Story?

Your money story may have more or fewer zeros attached to it than is the case for Paul and Anita. That doesn't matter. What matters is that you see the nuggets of wisdom embedded in their story, and actively test out whether you can apply that wisdom to your own situation. Both Anita and Paul are affected by old messages that no longer really apply, but have not yet been examined with adult insight and brought up to date. Therein lies the opportunity for using money as a powerful tool for creating life changes.

In Anita's case, still lingering is a childlike longing to "just be able to spend money" without the tight control that her childhood circumstances legitimately required. Also lingering in memory is a smoldering father – turned as a result of his illness from skilled meat cutter into organizer of home and hearth – who was capable of inflicting painful silences that affected the whole family. When Anita first talked about the prom dress story, she said "He didn't talk to my mother for three whole days." When she talked about it again, in relation to her reluctance to initiate financial decisions without Paul's prior approval, she said "My Dad didn't talk to us for three days." What matters here is not the literal truth of the original incident – whether the silence was inflicted only on her mother, or whether it spread to the whole household. What matters is the perception that lingers in Anita's memory: "My Dad got angry when we said we spent more than he approved of, and he didn't talk to us." That perception is the powerful force driving her behavior around money now.

Anita is living an old story; she needs to catch up with the disciplined, intelligent, playful person she is now. That means she no longer needs to use Paul as a "brake" on what she fears – that she will return to her spendthrift ways. She has the power to take that role inside herself, and exercise her own proven sense of good judgment. She also has the negotiating skill to present the changes she'd like to see to Paul and maintain the harmony of their marriage, which both cite as a value. She's proven that skill with the changes she's negotiated with her employer.

How can Anita initiate that catch-up? She can do so quite directly by picking one of the financial actions she longs to take: buying a new car, or installing a new dryer venting system in the house. She can look at her assets – if necessary, with the help of her financial advisor – decide how much to spend, and make the purchase. She can then let Paul know what she has done as part of an adult marital conversation, not as asking permission.

Will that cause Anita some short-term anxiety? Yes, she'll have to allow Paul his feelings, which may be different from hers. She'll also have to accept full responsibility for her own financial actions, be they good or misguided, and not pass the buck and the resulting animosity to Paul. Beyond the anxiety, taking thoughtful action will begin to give Anita a direct sense of her own power. Knowing the terrain of power, learning to use her financial assets to shape a future, is the challenge that faces Anita now.

In Paul's case, still lingering is the extreme frugality of a Depression-era role model, his father. Other than electronic devices – computers and the like – Paul buys almost nothing for himself. He drives a car, as he says, "until the wheels fall off." He speaks vaguely of "giving myself permission to start doing some of the things I've held off on," but is unable to name what one or two of those things might be. He's concerned about having enough money to cover all contingencies, and he continues to work very, very hard.

Paul needs to catch up with who he is now. He's no longer an upward-striving boy from a frugal family with high expectations for an eldest son's performance. Nor is he a young man frustrated by trying to please a woman in his first marriage who did not share his values or his work ethic. Paul is a successful professional man who has stayed with the cutting edge of new technology, has significant management skills, and who continues to add value despite a youth- oriented work culture that can readily disdain gray heads. Paul is also financially independent. He has "enough," says his financial advisor, to be secure, even if he doesn't feel secure. Paul and Anita work well together, live well together, and share numerous core values.

Paul has done the "money + success" side of the equation very well. He has that skill set mastered. He could continue to focus on amassing assets and professional credentials, but there's something he needs to do more. Now he needs to work on the more elusive "happiness" side of the equation. He needs to begin identifying what makes him happy, what are the things he's held off doing and could really begin doing right now. He has the health, the relationships, and the assets to support the outcome of such an inquiry.

What I'm proposing is a shift in the way Paul and Anita's joint treatment of assets has fallen into place over the years. I'm suggesting that each pause and develop a stronger sense of "this is my experience of money, and here's what I need to learn from money now," which will allow them to renegotiate the "we" of their money at a deeper level of intimacy. A strong and vital relationship isn't formed out of blending two different people into one monochromatic whole. Rather, a new level of intimacy can be achieved when two strong individuals respectfully negotiate what can and should be shared, and what needs to remain their separate work. Anita can support Paul in his new focus on what makes him happy, but she can't do that work for him. Paul can support Anita in wielding financial power, but he can't do that work for her.

Tackling money this way can be part of the joy of a long marriage, and of continuing to learn from experience until the day they die. Even after twenty-five years together, Paul and Anita can follow the thread of money to new places, to sides of themselves and each other that haven't been very visible before.

What If I'm Not Anywhere Near Integration?

Paul and Anita began their interview with me quite far along the path of integration. What if you're not anywhere near treating money as an ordinary part of your life? What if the steps you feel you can take are considerably lower risk than those that face Paul and Anita? Do smaller steps count?

When I first pushed Eric to take the plane while in Turkey, instead of the bus, he was quite angry with me. As he left my office, started his trip, and began to enjoy being in the country he loves, he gained some perspective. He recognized that my recommendation was just that: a recommendation. The choice remained his.

In the end, Eric did take the plane. When he returned from Turkey, he spontaneously traded in his ten-year-old rust bucket car and bought a relatively new Audi that he loves driving. He's made some larger charitable contributions, including one on behalf of the beleaguered Kurdish people, for whom he feels much empathy. He mustered enough courage to confront his financial advisor over what he perceived as her flippancy toward market dips, an event that causes him great anxiety and during which he needs more reassurance and less banter.

Eric is becoming hands-on with his money. He's shifted from denial and anxiety as the dominant ways he relates to money and moved into exploration. That represents enormous growth. In a very real sense, his very significant step is what this book is about: gathering the courage to move from where you are now to a place that's more satisfying. There are no "prizes" for getting to integration first. Nor are there any sanctions for "getting to ordinary" very late in life.

The woman with the large inheritance and I worked together for many months. I tried a number of strategies to help her reduce the sense of disruption the money had caused and to increase her sense that the inheritance was something her grandmother – out of love – wanted her to have. Nothing worked very well until I made a simple analogy. I asked if her grandmother had ever baked anything special when she came to visit. "Oh yes," she said immediately, "my grandmother baked the most wonderful brownies." I asked if she had ever rejected the brownies as being too much of a gesture of love, too overwhelming in their richness, more than she was entitled to have. A light dawned. "Do you think," she asked me, "that my grandmother meant the inheritance to be like that, something she created especially for me?" I said yes, I thought exactly that.

Despite this momentary breakthrough, my client continued to

experience her inheritance as troubling. She remained unable to find her own meaning for this very generous container – the inheritance – that her grandmother had gifted to her. I recommended that she work with a therapist to help uncover the deeper issues that I suspected were keeping her stuck, which she agreed to do.

Getting psychological help might seem like moving sideways, as if it makes money an even bigger issue instead of moving toward ordinary. That isn't true at all. This client's step to get the resources she needed to move on – in this case, psychological counseling – took significant courage, and represents real change.

Identifying Your Money Stage

If you don't feel that money is very well integrated into your life, here's a simple questionnaire to help you determine which money stage you might be in. Clearly, you can be experiencing the effects of more than one stage. What you're looking for is the dominant stage, the one that's most strongly influencing your behavior. You can tell that by picking the question you most identify with and seeing what stage is indicated. If you identify with several questions, is there consistency in the stage those questions describe? If not, think about which stage rings most true as characterizing your day-to-day experience.

1.   Do you often find yourself using terms like "always" or "never" about money? In other words, do you typically say things like "'I'm always thinking how I can make more money"? Or, might you say something like "I'll never depend on anyone other than myself for financial security, no matter what my situation is and no matter what the quality of the relationship might be"?

Anxiety. A "yes" answer to this question suggests you have a fear that you'll never have enough of a cushion to feel safe.

2.   Does the pursuit of money make you feel quite driven, even though you have enough money for your needs? Another way to ask yourself this question is: "Do I feel free, at least once in awhile, to stop

pressing so hard, to pass up a deal, to hold off on answering an email or voicemail so I can read or relax? Or, is my internal motor always revving?"

Anxiety. Think about this one. Are you saying you fear that no matter how hard you work, what you have won't last? Or, are you saying that you yourself aren't good enough, no matter how much you do? Could you be saying both?

3. Has money ever been used to control your choices or aspirations, and you could have protested but didn't?

Denial. Taking this position denies the power of money – your own, and the financial power others exert. It's a form of distancing from money, of pretending the "jolt" from the power source isn't there or isn't real, or only works in one direction – from the other person to you.

4. Have you ever been involved in a situation where money was used to intentionally harm someone, and you looked the other way even though you had the power to intervene?

Denial. Again, this is about pretending not to see the power of money. It's also about skill. When you deny or ignore the power of money, you don't develop the skills to hold fast or counter a power play when that kind of response is desperately needed.

5. Have you found that buying the things you've always wanted hasn't quite created the sense of happiness you crave?

Exploration. This behavior is about seeing whether or not money buys both containers and feelings. Remember that money does the first well enough, but not the second.

6. Have you ever intentionally concealed a money action you've taken, or the amount of money you have, in fear of the way someone might respond?

Denial. Money has a story of its own; that story is inescapably part of who you are. If you have to conceal who you are out of fear of the response, you're limiting your capacity for honesty and real intimacy.

7. Do you ever feel bored about your money, as if you've done

mostly everything money offers and you don't know what else there is to life?

Exploration. This is a common point people can reach while they're trying to figure out what money does. It can actually be very healthy – it can mean you've exhausted the effort to have money buy happiness and that you're ready to relate to money in a different way.

8.   Have you ever used the things money buys to keep you from getting close to people?

Denial. Using money as a way to protect yourself against intimacy is about pretending you're doing one thing when you're really doing another.

9.   Do you ever feel that no matter how much money you make, you can't be good enough or successful enough for your own standards or for the standards of people who matter in your life?

Anxiety. This one's about the fear that "I'll never be enough." This insidious mental tape often comes from unresolved hidden messages.

10. Are you excessively timid about taking charge of your money, out of fear you'll make a mistake, or because you believe that managing money isn't your role? Do you cover up your hesitation by saying things like "I just don't have a head for figures" or "I'm not interested in the money side – people are what I really care about"?

Denial. No healthy adult gets a "pass" on learning how to provide for oneself. You either do so directly, by becoming a revenue earner, or indirectly, by negotiating with someone to take care of you.

Based on everything you've read so far, how would you describe the stage that most strongly dominates your life right now? Remember that denial is primarily about pretending money doesn't exist or doesn't really matter. Anxiety is about the fear that you and/or your money will never be enough. Exploration is about getting "hands on" with your money – as a consumer, creator, investor, or all three. Integration is about letting money be money.

If you can't decide which stage is having the strongest influence on you, just pick one that resonates. You're the author of your own story; whatever you call your current stage will be good enough.

How Can You Move Closer to Integration?

Here are three common examples of people working with money stages, along with suggestions for how someone in this situation might begin to move closer to integration. You may or may not be able to find your own experience in these examples. If not, try to think how you might use what you read here as a jumping-off point to help you with what's happening in your life.

> Example #1: You hide from having inherited wealth, partly because you hate being hounded for money. You feel left out of the conversation when people with whom you serve on boards begin to talk about their work. You long to be considered just a regular person, so you can make friends without having to worry about hidden agendas.

Some people who grow up with inherited wealth have a lot of shame about being materially privileged, complicated by feelings of inadequacy about never having tested their abilities in the marketplace. Quite often they have the money, but not the complex skill set that accrued to whomever first created the fortune. They go into denial, fleeing from a hidden message that goes something like this: "Someone earned all this money, but not you. You couldn't possibly equal what that person once did, so don't even try. You're being taken care of, so what do you have to complain about?"

Work is about more than earning a living, which people of inherited wealth don't have to do. Work is about seeing how the public world might value what you bring to the table. That's useful information, whether or not you have a financial cushion behind you. Joanne Ciulla, author of *The Working Life,* talks about the role of work in even stronger terms:

> Work offers instant discipline, identity, and worth. It structures our time and imposes a rhythm on our lives. It gets us organized into various kinds of communities and social groups. And perhaps most important, work tells us what to do each day.

If you do feel uncomfortable with your money because you didn't earn it, if you sometimes feel "less than" people you know who work, try going down the path of finding work for pay. That action is a powerful way to dive headfirst into the most limiting consequence of inherited wealth: the difficulty measuring how you add value to the world. Go ahead and test yourself in the marketplace. You don't have to get an entry-level job trimming lettuce at the produce market or clerking at the drugstore. If your resources are big enough, you can do something substantial, like fund your own venture. Or you can, like Jacqueline Kennedy, find paid work you love – in the last years of her life she became a literary editor – and work for that reason, regardless of how little your salary adds relative to your net worth.

What's important here is not whether you actually wind up with a job. It's whether you actively confront your shame about not getting paid for what you do. Chris, a woman of inherited wealth in her mid-40's, was a successful community and political activist who used her money to create social change via those venues. Yet she had a nagging ambivalence about never having worked for pay as an adult. After working with her on that issue for a long time, I finally said, "So get a job." She did pursue several ideas for a launching a venture, exploring not only her interests but financing options and potential alliance partners. At a point not too far down the path of drafting her business plan, she decided – this time without ambivalence – that she liked being a community and political activist and a private investor. She's now able to pursue those endeavors without the emotional drag of feeling as if she'd be more credible to herself and to others if she worked.

> Example #2: No matter how much money you make, you feel you can't be successful enough to meet your own standards, or the standards of people who matter in your life.

The August 2000 *Inc.* magazine profiled a man they called "The Non-Stop, 24-7 CEO Salesman," known for personally selling more than almost anyone in his industry while running a fast-growing company at the same time. His day begins at 3:45 or 4:00 A.M. with a vigorous workout, continues at 8 A.M. with ten or eleven hours of straight meetings and presentations, then often ends with travel to another city. His personal goal is to sell $5 to 6 million dollars worth of product annually, while building a $100-million dollar company over ten years.

My clients aren't that wholeheartedly aboard the anxiety train, although some come close. The rub here is about external validation, the sense that you can't be OK until someone or something outside you – like your net worth number – says you're OK. Unfortunately, because of the seductiveness of money, winning that approval becomes more and more elusive. If you build a $100-million dollar company in ten years, and someone else builds a $200-million dollar company over the same time span, is he twice as smart and twice as good as you? That's the struggle for someone who can't feel successful, no matter how well he or she performs.

This is a difficult behavioral pattern to change. Sometimes our bodies demand it. The chief strategist for a global supply chain company had a major heart attack at age 40. Although inherited cardiac vulnerability may have been one component, so were stress, lack of exercise, and the inability to allow his body a respite from constantly pumping adrenaline. Sometimes the people around us draw the line in the sand; the divorce rate among this population tends to be high. Sometimes the frantic pace brings the individual to the edge of burnout, depression, self-injury, even to consider the possibility of suicide. That's often frightening enough to create an opening for change.

The ultimate goal here is to shift from external validation to an inner sense of what's important, what's good enough. That shift – and it's usually a long process – can't happen in an atmosphere of constant motion. It can only begin when people are willing to pause. In one case, I recommended that a CEO/head of new business development agree to shut down the new business pipeline for one month. Her company was growing faster than projects could be staffed, and there were many important management issues going by the boards while she was out cruising for new opportunities. The pause initially increased her anxiety, but did create an opening for change. She recognized that the business didn't come crashing down, even though there were no new accounts during that month. She recognized that she could stay attuned to the marketplace and to potential business opportunities without running out to close one. Most important, she was in the office all day for four weeks straight. People who had management issues that needed her attention were able to get time with her. Without the constant pressure of "I have to wind this conversation up and get to a prospect meeting," she was able to actually give her full attention to the problems and to the people affected by them.

> Example #3: You're timid about taking charge of your money because you fear doing something wrong, but you know you should be more attentive and on some level secretly want to be.

This is a person on the verge of becoming hands-on, and exploring what money can do.

No one gets to pass on learning to deal with money. We all have to pay bills, keep a roof over our heads, provide for a rainy day and for old age. If you depend on someone else to do those things for you, it's just that: dependency. In a healthy adult, ongoing dependency is a risky, one-down position. The problem is often a message that goes something like this: "You need me to take care of money for you, to act as a buffer against your worst impulses. You can't exercise that kind of discipline on your own. If I'm going to handle the money, I'll handle it; don't push me too hard over my decisions, or I'll get annoyed." A message like that can come from a spouse or partner, a trust officer, a financial or legal advisor, or another family member.

If you're timid because you're afraid of making a mistake, think of handling money the way you think of car mechanics. To keep a car on the road you don't have to understand in depth what goes on under the hood. You do have to know enough to keep the car gassed up, get oil changes and routine maintenance, and pay attention to proper tire inflation. You do have to find a good mechanic, and ride herd over what that person does. It's the same with money. You don't have to read *The Wall Street Journal* every day, or use complex options strategies, or become a commodities trader. You do have to master, and act on, the basics of building financial independence. Save regularly, and begin at an early age. Don't let your savings linger in low-interest financial products; choose investment vehicles that offer a rate of return that allows you to build capital. Avoid high-interest consumer debt. Diversify your assets among classes of investments. Use tax-advantaged investments when they are available to you. Don't risk more than you can afford to lose; don't risk less than you must in order to build an asset base. Keep a long-term perspective. Learn to read statements. Pay attention; if your portfolio tanks, deal with it. Find good financial advisors who can take time with you to explain these concepts in more depth.

Look at learning about money the same way you've learned about everything else in your life: as an exciting developmental process. Try this as a beginning behavioral change: take a modest amount of money under your wing, and experiment. As you learn and gather confidence, take charge of more – at least from the standpoint of really understanding and agreeing conceptually with what an advisor lays out. If that requires renegotiating with your spouse, partner, trust officer, financial advisor, attorney, or accountant, do so. If you make a mistake and lose money on a particular financial move, so be it. Figure out what you need to do differently and get back into the game. Trust that your best effort will be good enough.

Most importantly, talk about what you're doing financially with people who have similar interests and who are "hands-on" with their money too. Ask questions. Develop a forgiving attitude toward yourself; not even the most high-flying of market gurus picks winners 100% of the time.

Where Are We?

You now have the tools and perspective you need to go on to the remaining chapters, where we'll tackle money's hardest questions and begin to examine some life-changing decisions. You've gotten a sense of your own money story, both past and present. You've looked at the power of money as a thread in shaping who you are. Perhaps you've broken through the silence that typically surrounds money and have begun to talk about your experience with others. You've looked at various stages of relating to money, and picked the one that's most currently true for you.

Remember that experiencing different stages of relating to money is developmentally normal. The stage you're in now reflects what you've seen and done and currently face, not your intelligence or character. Figuring out where you are now is a prerequisite to moving toward integration, toward letting money be money. When money becomes a regular part of what you focus on during the course of a day, you have the chance to develop useful skills. You learn to cope better with money's more challenging aspects, like how to use the power money always conveys.

CHAPTER FOUR

"How Do You Use the Power Money Always Conveys?"

IF YOU HAVE MONEY, you can command a coveted place in rooms where big decisions are made. You can find your way to the legislative arena and have a say in which initiatives are going to be funded and which will die untested. You can set priorities for a company, a university, a family, or a relationship. You can resurrect failing enterprises. You can buy the best professional services on the market. You can distinguish yourself from others by the way you dress, the car you drive, the restaurants you are comfortable eating in, and the studied casualness with which you can commit thousands or tens of thousands of dollars. That's what I mean when I say that money is a source of power: the power to differentiate yourself, to gain access, and to prevail.

If you have power, you can get money. People will give it to you. That's the essence of political fundraising. Although it's more efficient to run for elective office with your own money – as have presidential candidate Steve Forbes and Senator Jon Corzine of New Jersey – you don't have to come from wealth in order to win an election. You simply have to convey to moneyed people that you understand their needs and will protect those needs once you are in office. Then "OPM," or "other people's money," will kick in. If you project an aura of power in business, you can get money. Again, people will give it to you. Josh is 24, a Harvard graduate, a brilliant and personable guy, former CEO of an Internet media company and now the proverbial dot.com millionaire. To raise money for his venture he bootstrapped his own savings, an investment from his father, and personal credit cards. Of his success at getting an initial stake, he says, "I'm amazed at how much credit was extended to a then-22 year old with no credit history whatsoever. It was April 1999 when we started the company, and we had a term sheet on the table in late August from a group of angel investors. We figured the money would see us through until May of 2000, and we sold the company in March 2000. We never had to raise any more money after those first rounds." Even in the over-heated atmosphere for Internet companies in 1999 and early 2000, money didn't flow to everyone. Money flowed to those who conveyed that they were on their way to making a big footprint on the world. That's what I mean when I say that power begets money.

Money and power, in these situations at least, are joined at the hip. Money and power have a symbiotic relationship in which the presence of one calls forth the other. There are other kinds of power, more akin to personal power, where the role of money is less clear and where a money story may be less explanatory. There's power in overcoming the instinct for self-preservation and thrusting oneself forward in combat. There's power in leaving an abusive relationship. There's power in holding your ground on something you believe in, and power in walking away from a foolish fight. Those experiences of power are important in the world, and important to acknowledge here. They create a fuller picture of "power," and help create a con-trast with the kind of power that is our focus in this book.

We're looking at harnessing the power of money. "How do I wield money's power?" is one of the most crucial things for us to explore, simply because money has such a profound influence over most peo-ple's behavior. Money creates power in a way that's analogous to the way falling water creates electricity. Such power begs to be used, but any power source can be used for good or for ill. Electricity can illu-minate Third World villages; it can also be used to torture people. Money can create access, innovation, and opportunity. Money can educate, fuel discoveries, and initiate healing. Money can also be used to control, to exclude, and to destroy.

Flat-out making money is much easier that learning to wield its power wisely. We're responsible to each other, because of our common humanity, for the ways we use the power of money. We all hold that accountability whether or not we consider ourselves "big money players." Anyone in our American culture who has a checkbook, a credit card, an investment statement, medical benefits, or a pension plan is an insider when it comes to money, not an outsider. People who are big players have big accountability for the way money is used in our society. People who struggle to make ends meet have fewer chips to play, a smaller sphere of influence, and more limited accountability.

In a culture where we don't talk openly about money, how do we learn to harness money's power, either as individuals or as people striving to make a big footprint in a public setting? What does it mean in each case to handle that power well? There's no single, entirely successful model. The power of money is too complicated for that.

Exercising Ordinary Power

At the very least, those with any access to money's power have to learn not to ride roughshod over the hopes, aspirations, rights and identities of others. That's what I call "wielding power without whacking people".

> Daniel is a ceramic artist with a small following of collectors who buy his work. He's also an assistant professor in a community college art department with a salary of $28,000. His wife, a senior corporate executive, makes more than six times as much. "I could handle it better if she made twice as much," he told me ruefully," but six times? What must people think of me?" Daniel came to see me because his department was being eliminated, which would soon end his most reliable source of income. No problem, his wife had briskly retorted. One of her colleagues owed her big time for the amount of business she had sent his way, and could no doubt be prevailed upon to create a job somewhere in his company's graphic arts department – at a decent salary, she took pains to add. Daniel's face, as he reported the conversation, was glum. "How can she discount how much I love my work? How can she not understand that I have no desire to do some made-up job she gets for me? Besides, I don't even do graphic arts."

Whack.

Marie graduated from college with an elementary education degree, but she and her husband had their first child before she ever entered a classroom. Because certification requirements have been upgraded, she would now need a master's degree before she could expect to land a teaching job – the only work for which she feels remotely qualified. Her husband, a successful lawyer, was having a not-very-well-concealed affair. Confronted, he told her that if she filed for divorce he would fight her tooth and nail for the children. No lawyer in town would represent her, he blustered, because they were all his friends. She came to see me to explore whether there was any kind of work she could land immediately that would pay enough to partially support their three children and fight her husband for divorce at the same time. He would not, she was sure, make collecting even transitional alimony and child support easy.
Whack.

I've known Daniel and his wife professionally for many years. She was not, in my view, conscious of riding roughshod over her husband. In her work role, she is called on by the hour to wade into problems and drive for resolution. Her ability to find quick and smart solutions is partly responsible for her high salary and her status within the company. She has far more experience in her industry than the members of her team, and if pressed, would admit she trusts her own solutions more than theirs. Daniel's situation, as she was ultimately able to acknowledge, was not "her work problem." Daniel's situation was his. When he came home from a departmental meeting earlier that month and had shared the bad news, he hadn't been asking her to act, only to show support and empathy. He had shown initiative by coming to see me to explore what he might do moving forward. By temperament, Daniel is more a patient shaper – a true ceramic artist – than a driving problem solver. As a couple, he and his wife had enough income so that the loss of his teaching salary would not put their lifestyle in jeopardy. There was time for a solution more akin to his natural style to emerge.

Daniel needed breathing room. With his consent, our early conversations expanded to include his wife. In those meetings, Daniel had to flex relationship skills he hadn't used much before. He had to take back the power to solve the problem, and make it his own. Over several sessions, he and his wife agreed on boundaries. Daniel would continue to actively pursue options, understanding that he might have to face some hard career choices if he wanted to replace his teaching salary with another predictable source of income. He voluntarily offered to talk more openly with his wife as his thinking progressed, knowing that what she experienced as "his moody silence" while he was pondering problems was apt to drive her crazy. He agreed to be explicit in asking for her help if help was wanted, and equally explicit in saying when he was simply asking her to listen. She, in turn, agreed to let Daniel be Daniel. We had some humorous, and poignant, exchanges about how "opposites attract" in a marital relationship. Because she loved Daniel, she expressed a willingness to flex a relationship skill of her own that had gone mostly unused. She agreed to temper the blunt force of her problem-solving abilities in the interests of giving Daniel room to solve his career dilemma in his own way. With the agreement in place, Daniel and I returned to a one-on-one conversation about his professional future.

Surely it will surprise no one to hear that the agreement was more easily arrived at than lived. Without being distracted by having to push against his dynamo of a wife, Daniel had to confront the reality of having chosen a vocation that doesn't pay well. Money – and what the people around him thought of his ability to earn money – mattered more to him than he had thought. Although the two had agreed prior to their marriage that all marital assets were "theirs," and it wouldn't matter who put what amount into the common pot, it turned out that it did matter to both of them. Daniel was bothered by the difference between his wife's ability to provide income for them, and his own. She, in turn, was bothered by his seeming lack of ambition, which she had concluded was the case from Daniel's willingness to work for a salary that was less than "decent."

Clearly, the unresolved issue of Daniel's next career step had given rise to significant marital tensions. Daniel and his wife agreed that the first priority was to get him situated with a new source of income. Then, they would follow up on my referral to a marital therapist who could help them work through the relationship issues.

Working through both sets of problems would allow the two to take their relationship to a new and deeper level of intimacy.

"Whacking" behavior is very likely to arise when there is an imbalance of financial power. Such an imbalance can occur between spouses or partners, between a company's highly-paid sales staff and its back-office operations, between parents and adult children, between friends, alliance partners, employers and employees, or among business competitors. Whacking behavior can also occur when there is a differing level of skill in applying monetary clout, a clash of values or priorities, too few strategies for resolving conflicts, or too many possible solutions and too little time to choose among them.

The goal is to equalize the power equation as much as possible. That doesn't mean stripping legitimate power away from the one who seems to begin with the stronger hand. Daniel's wife was entitled to keep her much-vaunted problem-solving skills and her forward-thrusting style, as long as she didn't use them to ride roughshod over Daniel. Equalizing power does mean supporting the one perceived to have the weaker position in asserting his or her own needs. For Daniel to move beyond feeling overwhelmed by his wife's strong response, he had to step up and claim responsibility for his career trajectory and for his own way of solving problems.

Sometimes the power difference is not resolved. The parties simply agree to move back from the edge, and the whacking behavior goes into "sleep mode." The crisis subsides until awakened again by a new event. Marie and I worked together for many months on what career options she might consider, what supportive services might help her in the battle with her husband, and on what it might be like to take on financial responsibility for herself and share financial responsibility for the children. She and her husband had married right out of college; she had never, even for a few months, been financially responsible for herself, and the thought terrified her. While Marie and I were working together, she and her husband were receiving counseling from their pastor. In that setting her husband had agreed to temper his belligerent behavior and to stop the affair. Both agreed on their strong commitment to the well-being of their children. Even without a reaffirmation of her husband's commitment to her, Marie told me she was simply too frightened to follow through with the divorce. She would rather put up with what she now knew to be a long pattern of marital infidelities until the children were out of the home; then she might reconsider her options.

Following the story of money and power doesn't lead to a particular resolution, only to a truer definition of the problem and a more intentional choice of outcome. You get to pick what you think you can best live with.

Once you've gone beyond the first step in using the power of money well – restraining the temptation to run over other people – you are ready to think more proactively. Money has equivalent power to create goodness, or pain. If you have a power source available to you in the form of money, what good can you make happen?

A young woman was deeply concerned about her best friend's prolonged depression. Knowing that the friend's medical plan did not cover mental health services, the young woman stepped up and paid for counseling out of her own pocket. The intervention, the friend told her, was literally life-saving.

A mid-life school administrator with modest savings was shocked when his brother – ten years younger than he – suffered a massive heart attack. Without asking for an accounting of his brother's obligations and debts, the older man quietly sent a check for $10,000 to "help take away any financial worries that might get in the way of your recovery."

A mid-life professional couple without children of their own have taken on a new identity as "Big Momma and Poppa" to various young adults who have landed on their doorstep. "If we have the financial and other resources to give these kids what they need at crucial points in their lives, so be it. Ours isn't a conventional family, but what is?"

Katherine, the architect you met in an earlier chapter, provides her highly specialized services on a pro bono basis to programs that enhance the economic independence of women and girls. Her most recent project was supervising the renovation of a nonprofit incubator for small women-owned businesses. She stepped in at a time when the sponsoring agency had nearly run out of money, and without her donation of services might have had to abandon the project.

Exercising Public Power

The power of money plays out on a personal level in all of these ways, and more. If you earn two or three times your best friend's salary, how do you negotiate which restaurant you'll choose for dinner? If one of your adult children is far more successful than the other, how do you arrange your bequests? If your affluent mother-in-law "buys" your children's attention with lavish gifts, how do you balance the scales with regard to the children's other grandma?

The power of money also plays out in the public arenas where some of us strive to leave a big and lasting footprint on the world. Josh's exercise of public power has been distinctive because of his youth, the relative speed of his attaining millionaire status, and his luck with timing. Three weeks after he led the sale of the company, the whole market for Internet ventures plummeted. Since then, the value of his restricted stock has been on a roller coaster, with the trend mostly down. Market value on the day he and I talked was around $10 a share – still making him worth three to four million dollars. By temperament Josh is quick, focused, intense, and not at all sure he even likes the word "power." He prefers to focus on the accomplishments of the team.

Josh's exercise of public power has been good: he created a company that provides a profitable service to both businesses and consumers. The company offers challenging jobs at fine salaries to a growing number of employees. And he leveraged that initial success into a sale that brought his young company more financial stability and a larger future.

Art's exercise of public power has been distinctive because he's been able to sustain the ride far longer than most of his peers. He's done that by simply refusing not to be a player any more. At 70, Art remains an active power broker and deal maker. Retired as chairman of a major financial institution, Art no longer wields operating authority. His power is a function of his ability to spot deals, find capital, and bring to bear his "golden Rolodex" on behalf of various Wall Street firms with whom he now maintains a consulting relationship. By temperament Art is invariably gracious and mannered; he wields power like a rapier, cutting agreements that are smooth, lucrative, and finely assembled.

Art's exercise of public power has been good: he's created real value in the form of well-constructed deals, and he's been willing to mentor countless younger men coming along behind him. He's also served his community by sharing his expertise on various issues related to economic development.

Katherine's exercise of public power has been distinctive because she has the top job, is the mother of grown children and a grand-mother, and can easily hold her own with "the boys" without losing herself as a woman. Like many women in senior executive positions, she's had to juggle all of those roles successfully to be where she is. At 58, Katherine is the operating CEO of a mid-sized liberal arts college, an active power broker, and a deal maker. Hired to turnaround the struggling institution, part of Katherine's many-pronged strategy was to land a contract that brought a major sports team to the revamped college athletic facilities for summer training camp. She then added an academic major in sports management, which converted a substantive public relations opportunity into a real draw for new students. By temperament, Katherine is bold. Like the home run hitters of my childhood team, the Yankees, Katherine's power lies in her savvy about swinging for the bleachers when the opportunity is right, and in her cool ability to walk away when the deal does not bring enough benefit to her institution.

Katherine's exercise of public power has been good; she's revitalized an institution that had sunk so low financially "they weren't even buying grass seed." She's also kept the mission of the institution intact. "I strive to make this a first-generation college experience. Sixty percent of our kids are the first in their families to go to college. I never want us to become a country club. Those young people who have money are never hungry enough to achieve what the kid who doesn't have money achieves."

Comfort with our public exercise of power is something we grow into over time as we shape the role to fit our skills and temperament. Josh, Art, and Katherine are very different kinds of power brokers. They are all, by any standards, professionally successful.

And how, might you ask, does one shape such a powerful role?

Power Stories, Too, Reach Back in Time

Just as our overall money story reaches back into our childhood, so too does the link between money and power. Understanding how your beliefs came to operate in their present form is essential before you begin to tinker with those beliefs. For Katherine, the connection between money and power was made by the age of six or seven.

> I grew up in an immigrant community on Manhattan's West Side. We lived in a walk-up flat. My community spanned about four blocks in either direction. We were mostly Italian and Irish, then Middle or Eastern European and German. There were gang wars, not in the sense that you would see on TV, but there were certainly turf issues, name-calling. But all of the people in that immigrant community understood money and the power of money, and understood that education was the avenue. When I was six or seven, money meant the ability to treat friends. The candy store was on the corner, and very often one had to buy one's friendships. If you bought candy and distributed it, you had friends for at least three or four hours.

Because it's more abstract, the concept that the power to spend money not only buys attention but also sets one apart is likely to come later. Art grew up in a very small town, where his father was a Main Street merchant and his mother a homemaker. Art could have stayed in town and taken over the store. Instead, he graduated from a Midwestern university and headed for Wall Street, where he was hired as a trainee.

> The first week I was there one of my fellow trainees came over and said to me "We're Brooks Brothers here – you really ought to take a look at your clothes." I trudged down to Brooks Brothers and looked at the suits. They cost $300-$400, which was as much as I made in a month. I didn't have it. I went to talk with one of the back office folk and he said "Oh, come with me." We went to a 7th Avenue loft where there were whole piles of suits that looked exactly like Brooks Brothers. They were $25

apiece. For another 25 cents you could buy a Brooks Brothers label and have it sewn in. For 35 cents you could buy a Savile Row label with the little red lines on it. I remember deciding that if they were Brooks Brothers I wanted to be Savile Row. That was the beginning of a feeling that I always wanted to differentiate myself from the crowd. I also sensed at that point that there was an attraction to having money. It occurred to me that it was not a bad pursuit, so I pursued it.

Sometimes wielding power in the business world means figuring out for yourself the full scope of what power entails. When I asked Josh what it meant to him to exercise the power that comes with being a CEO, he said, "When I think of power, I think of someone like a head of a corporation or the head of government who wants something to happen and it happens. I don't really think of money being the number one thing that drives that kind of power. I'd like to think there was something having to do with personality and the hard work ethic of the team that had a lot to do with us commanding power. Startup is a lot about smoke and mirrors and getting everyone to believe in a vision. It's only when everyone's believing your pie-in-the-sky that the myth becomes a reality."

Power in public settings can have an undeniably hard edge. Grasping that, too, comes at an early age. Katherine remembers going to a school where "there weren't enough seats for all the kids in the class. The kids who got there first got to sit down. Kids who got there first got the books. There weren't enough books. I didn't want to share. It was very early in my life that I figured out that you have to make what you want happen. It's not going to happen for you. You have to make it happen." Later in life, the hard edge is reflected in Art's response to my question about putting a company in play:

The company's role in the social fabric of a community would not matter at all to me. The game would matter. If a company is put into play, if a person is put into play, it's generally because of a deficiency. No one is ever put into play out of strength. Although I don't agree that greed is good, I do accept the fact that there is a Darwinian motion to companies and to people. If you're in play – which is a form of weakness on your part – then you deserve to be in play and whatever replaces you will be better than you.

Power in public settings sometimes cuts people a little slack, but not much, and not for long. The decision of whether to give someone a break has a lot to do with the financial position of the organization. At the height of his career as a CEO, Art headed a highly profitable financial institution.

> We bought another bank in which the CEO was quite elderly. My people wanted to get rid of him immediately. I discussed it with his wife, and she felt being let go would kill him. He wasn't well, and it seemed as if we could wait a year or so to do something. I did wait. The decision was financially costly. Everybody who wanted to get rid of him was absolutely right from a shareholder point of view. It was something I could not and would not do.

Turnaround does not offer that kind of wiggle room. No more than six weeks after coming on board, Katherine grasped the full measure of the college's financial crisis:

> When I realized how bad things were, I immediately fired the entire senior staff. They were the ones who had been here for the last twenty years, and the ones who had gotten us here. Had they had solutions, they would have implemented them already.

Start-up means learning to juggle interests that sometimes compete – what's good for the business, and what's good for an individual who works for the business. Part of strategy to accelerate the rapid growth of Josh's company was to acquire other firms.

> I was very involved with another company that we had just acquired. We integrated a lot of what they were doing into our operation and then just shut them down. I had to let some people go. I didn't know their personal financial situations, but obviously it was very tough. You have to look at it from two perspectives. One is what is in the best interest of the company. Then you go to the flip side, the more touchy-feely side, and think about the impact on the person, whether you should make the extra effort and try to keep them in the firm even though in some cases they're underperforming. In the end, a decision has to be made in a balance of those two things, and it's very tough.

Not surprisingly, the exercise of public power maps to the core values of the culture of success. The first of those is speed. As Art reflected on the changes in deal making that have occurred over the decades in which it has been his professional focus, he said, "In dealing with Wall Street firms now, particularly when relationships do not mean very much but deals mean everything, there's a laziness, a desire to reach for the low-hanging fruit, for the instant gratification. You can't build a posture of putting something in play over a two-year period. It's really got to be something that can happen now. We live in a very much now world."

The second core value is running at the head of the pack. Katherine began her professional life as a second-grade teacher. "I saw the ladder. In every profession there's a ladder. I saw the ladder in public education and started climbing. Then I started another career ladder in higher education because it was easier to jump. You could jump several levels in higher ed, and the hours weren't as long. Every time I moved, it was for a career opportunity. Now I have the CEO job I wanted."

The third core value is financial success. Katherine's total compensation package is in the six-figure range, including use of the president's residence, a car lease, and other benefits. Art has a solid seven-figure net worth. Josh is a young millionaire.

The fourth core value is making a big and visible footprint on the world. Josh began a small company and grew it in less than two years to be part of a major public corporation. He likes start-up; he's good at start-up. "After I go to business school, or if I choose not to go to business school, I'd want to start company #2. I don't know what #2 will be, but I had a great time doing this one. The part I like the most is the start-up phase, so that's what I'd want to relive." Katherine creates her big impact in part by using college scholarships to shape student values. "There are lots of opportunities to use money in a way to change the lives of others, and I recognize that very clearly. We spend a lot of money here on scholarships – not for grade-point average, but for service and for character attributes. This institution has always advocated strongly for students to perform community service, but I put the money to it – full $25,000 scholarships. As soon as I attached the money, the value of service was quantifiable. I don't believe I corrupt the value of service by rewarding it financially. What' s wrong with rewarding valuable behavior or characteristics? We do it in every other part of life."

Art's big footprint has to do with his "golden Rolodex", his ability to call on powerful people around the country and get a desired response.

> Over the last thirty or forty years I have never refused to see someone in an executive position who was unhappy, and to ask myself: Is there something I could do to help him? My theory was "It could be me," and I meant it. Over that time period I have placed many people in positions of authority where I had something to do with their success. This was because I wanted to, and because it was very deliberately self-serving. Throughout my career I've been assisted by people who said "Hey, he was there for me. I ought to be there for him." I don't mind using that at all. I don't have any hesitation calling someone I made a CFO and saying "I could use some help now." If he says "no" so be it, but I don't mind asking because I've paid my dues with him.

The Leverage Points, the Price to Pay, and the Rewards

Successfully exercising power in big public settings has to do with two key elements: choosing as your focus something that can grow big, and being astute about picking the precise leverage points that will ignite growth. Art's chosen focus is financial deal making. Here's how he describes the leverage point that makes it work:

> You always have to start with the self-interest of the person you're dealing with. Then, you have to make that self-interest work for you. The essence of power is finding out what someone really wants and giving it to him for your own personal benefit. If you do that, everyone is happy. I've rarely been in deals where someone has walked away tremendously unhappy – and those cases were mainly about emotional issues, not financial issues. On balance, the wisdom is finding the self-interest of the individual and somehow manipulating it in a manner that is to your mutual benefit.

Katherine's most recent focus has been turnaround. Here's how she describes the leverage points that made her situation work:

> I immediately hired a CFO, someone who was a combination of good basic accounting and the ability to think. I needed someone to help me think about money, to help me think my way out of this mess. Then I hired an enrollment manager; I had to get the fannies through the doors to sit in the classrooms. I also made the decision that I was going to pay my new senior staff 1 ½ times the going rate, because I was recruiting people into a high-risk environment – a ship that looked like it was going to go down. Then I went to the board and told them we couldn't make it by cutting expenses. We had cut all there was to cut. We had to spend, and spend big. The money was in the endowment, and we had to take it out and give the appearance of looking good, of thriving. People would only come here if it looked as if we were going to succeed.

Josh's focus has been start-up. Here's how he describes the leverage points that made his company work:

> You need a decent idea – but ideas are a dime a dozen. The idea of our company, the business model, has changed so much since the day we started – and still changes every day. The most important things in starting a company are people who are smart, people who can be a jack-of-all-trades, people who are flexible about changing roles, and people who can command respect. If you're going to be leaders of a company and people don't respect you, then it will never work.

For all the exhilaration of being successful in making an impact on the world, there is a price to pay. Katherine describes that price most succinctly.

> You pay the price on different levels. You pay the price on a personal level, in your personal relationships. You pay the price in your day-to-day life because what you're doing, the problem you're solving, what you're thinking about, is with you all the time. It never goes away. You pay the price in your lifestyle. I have a lifestyle that would be the envy of most. However, it's an unbalanced lifestyle. It's unbalanced in terms of health. It's unbalanced in terms of love relationships. It's unbalanced in the way I spend money. It's unbalanced in terms of where I put my time and energy. I wouldn't trade all of that, but any powerful CEO has an unbalanced lifestyle, and that is the price.

There is a price to pay on many levels; there are also multiple levels of rewards. Josh describes himself as very happy with his friends and family and very happy with his career. He's financially successful, although not yet totally sure how to place his wealth in a relative context. He recognizes that his stock holdings place him in the top 1% of the population in terms of assets. Yet he grew up in an affluent community and knew people who were in the top 0.1%, or even the top 0.01%. The definition of being "rich" in such a context, in Josh's mind, "might or might not be me – I don't know."

Art describes himself as "having given my wife and daughters a good life and that was my goal." He also expresses delight that his wife of thirty-eight years is still part of his life. "I always thought I was a very difficult person to live with, and I really couldn't understand why anyone would want to live with me. I find it quite miraculous that I've behaved myself sufficiently that she still hangs around." He speaks of relative wealth in an interesting way: "Enough" is the point at which people no longer question your motivations. "There's a pecking order in money and wealth. The Rockefellers reached a point historically where they were immune to the question of motive. Bill Gates sets up a $21 billion dollar fund and is doing marvelous things in education and health – yet people say he's trying to do something about Microsoft's anti-trust problem. Maybe he is, but I doubt it. If Bill Gates' grandson is chairman of the Gates Foundation in 2060, no such motives will be attributed to him. Time does create different scenarios."

Katherine's rewards, and her sense of having enough money, power, and success, are tied to a certain understanding of happiness.

I know if I have enough money, because I can evaluate my money with everyone else's. I know if I have enough power because I can measure it the same way. I can't measure my happiness. There's no price tag on it, no quantitative level to it. So, I never know if I'm happy, or happy enough. I have to rely on other measures, like the absence of pain, or stress, or self-destructive behavior. Right now I'm pretty happy. I like my job. I'm making money that I think is appropriate to my effort. I think we are successful as an institution and will continue to be. I'm comfortable in my environment. I'm involved in a romantic relationship. Most of my women friends are comfortable. I've got everything compartmentalized nicely; there's not a lot of slopover. That, to me, is happiness.

What Does All This Mean for You?

We live in a culture that quickly jumps to analyze the behavior and motivations of people like Josh, Art, and Katherine, and moves equally quickly to express judgments. That's not the point of these stories. The point is to give you some examples of how other people harness the power money conveys, then ask you to look at the way you use money's power in your public and private life.

If you're like most of us, your money story serves you better in some aspects of life than in others. If you want to change that, you have to locate the spots where things aren't working well, and find ways to shift your behavior. That's the point of grappling with money's hardest questions.

The stories do help you figure out your own relationship with power. The following questions help you put that relationship into words, so you can see and hear what you're doing, and make some assessments about your choices.

Have you made the intentional choice to go after the kind of power money brings?

Katherine saw the career ladder, and began to climb. Josh saw the potential to build a company, and set up shop. Art liked attention and power, and saw making money as a key to getting both.

Are you on an equivalent path? Do you acknowledge that your path is an intentional choice? Why have you made that choice? What do you expect this particular container – the exercise of public power – to do for you? How do you expect your exercise of power to benefit others – or do you? Big power carries big voltage – what are you doing to equip yourself with the skills to handle power at this level? If you've chosen not to go after public power, why have you made that decision? Are you more or less happy with the decision today, compared with how you felt when you made it? Can you say why?

What's your basic style of exercising power?

Katherine – and Daniel's wife – are blunt-force power brokers. That doesn't mean lacking in subtlety or sophistication, or that they can't back away when called to do so. It does mean their basic style is to swing for the home run. Art wields power with great finesse. I asked how he handled it when someone tried to get him to hire a person he considered unqualified. Here was his response:

I'd like to say that out of a sense of integrity and a sense of responsibility to my own position I just said "no." That wasn't true. What I generally did was research the individual who was being recommended to me. Then I would let his champion know what was wrong. I would cut the legs out from under the candidate by giving his champion information that hadn't come to light but that I knew from experience would keep the person from being successful. I'd use whatever tool I needed. I would present it as saving the champion from embarrassment. I'd say, "If I take him, he'll fail for those reasons, and that will reflect badly on you. So I'm not taking him, because I want to protect you from that."

Josh is a sheer-intensity power broker, a person willing and able to convince financial backers, vendors, clients, employees, the media – and his fellow founders – that the smoke and mirrors were real until the company was far enough along to actually be real.

In what kinds of settings does your style of exercising power work best?

Have you picked a professional setting that's a good fit with your style? In other words, if you're a blunt-force power broker, you're not trying to succeed at being the abbot of an order of contemplative monks, are you? Do you work best with other people whose style is similar to yours, or does that create too much conflict and competition? How patient are you with people whose style is very different? If you're a finesse power bro-ker, how do you deal with blunt-force types? If you're a sheer-intensity type, how do you deal with finesse power brokers whose moves may seem too deliberate and behind-the-scenes? Is there anything you can envision doing that will increase the range of people with whom you can work successfully?

If you want to make a big impact on the world, have you focused professionally on something that is big, or can get big?

Katherine runs a college, Art helps put together big deals, and Josh runs a company. If you want to make a big impact of the kind money makes possible, you too have to go for some-thing big. Small, niche, or boutique operations may be highly satisfying professionally, but they may or may not make enough of an impact to meet the "large footprint" criteria. Daniel creates fine ceramic pieces. The work has a big impact on him, and on the people who collect what he makes. In terms of "footprint on the larger world," how many nationally known ceramic artists can you name?

If you want to run at the head of the pack, do you have the neces-sary resilience to weather the competition?

The famous bell-shaped curve tells us that in any population there will be relatively few at the leading edge, a large middle, and another relative few trying their best to keep up at all. If you want to be in the first group, the performance competi-tion will be intense and can get ugly. Do you want it? Do you know why or why not? If you do want it, do you have the skills to hold your own?

Are you clear about the price of exercising public power, and clear about your willingness to pay that price?

At the very least, exercising power on a big stage means an unbalanced life. There may be other implications. As you look at your life, what has been the cost of the way you exercise power? On whom has that cost primarily fallen? Have you been as clear about the cost with the people you ask to share your life, especially your spouse or partner and children? If you're getting a lot of the rewards and others are getting a lot of the fallout, what do you need to do to change that?

Are you sure you want the kind of power money brings, more than any other kind of power?

Earlier we talked about containers, which are constructs that hold our aspirations. Understand that the power created by money very much fits the definition of a container. When we go after money's power, we expect something to happen for us. If you focus largely on gaining that kind of power, every ounce of time and energy you can bring to bear is likely to be consumed in the effort. You may not have enough left over to experience other kinds of power: mentoring a child who isn't yours, being a friend to someone who is mentally ill, serving in a hospice or soup kitchen or homeless shelter. Make sure the kind of power you're seeking is the kind of power you want. If not, do you need to look for a different container?

On the personal side of exercising power, how good are you at not running over people?

I can immediately recognize someone who goes through life with what I call a "ruler of the universe" mentality. At a recent conference in which I participated, the speaker asked us to break into groups of five to seven and spend time discussing our reactions to his talk. Immediately a member of my group began to organize us: summarizing what points she thought we should focus on, then telling us how long each of us should speak, and in what order. She turned to me and said brightly, "Let's hear from you first." My evil twin comes out in these situations. I simply said "No," then fell silent. The effect was as I had hoped. She was startled into silence, the rest of the group relaxed, and we all began a more spontaneous conversation. If it has been your custom to use your personal power in a way that's domineering, can you try flexing a less-used skill, such as the capacity to listen? Your world might begin to look very different.

If you don't consider yourself powerful, are you looking at the full definition of "power" and claiming your place accordingly?

The examples we've been looking at show power reaching outward – with bluntness, with finesse, with intensity. There are other kinds of power that we often fail to see as power because they're turned inward. The power of love and the willingness to nurture are positive examples of such inner-directed power. I once visited a classroom at the Mary Cariola Children's Center, a fine facility dedicated to caring for children with severe traumatic brain injury and other major developmental disabilities. In this classroom, the most seriously affected children were lying on cushions, most curled into a fetal position, being fed twenty-three hours a day through tubes. To my untrained eye, the children offered no signs of communicating with their caregivers or even being aware of their surroundings. I asked the teachers whether they could detect a response from their young charges. "Oh yes," they assured me. "We can tell immediately if a child is responding to us with passive resistance or passive acceptance." That response was an astonishing illustration of the power of empathy.

The power of silence can be a more negative example of power turned inward. I once worked with a senior leadership team whose decision model was based on consensus. One of the team members, who had a critically important operational role in the company, remained silent at all leadership team meetings. She exerted disproportionate power in the group because so much energy was diverted to trying to figure out what she was thinking. Other examples of power turned inward are the power of chaos, in which someone will have such a large emotional reaction to any suggested change that team members decide it's hardly worth proposing anything, and the power of victimhood, where someone will act as if any action of the group is intended to undermine him or her. Silence, chaos, and victim behavior all tend to be very powerful in shutting down the forward motion of a group. If you haven't previously considered yourself powerful but you do often get your way, be honest with yourself. How is that happening? Is your exercise of power – although it might be working for you – really the best way for you to contribute in a relationship or on a team?

Finally, if you accept money as a power source that can be used equally for good or for ill, how are you using whatever level of power you have?

Power isn't exercised in a vacuum; our exercise of power affects others, even in cases where people seem mostly self-focused. Is the way you use power today consistent with your deepest beliefs and values? Have you looked recently at what those beliefs and values are? If not, what has to change? What might be reason enough to motivate you to change? What do you think might happen over time if you don't do some things differently? What do you hope might happen if you do?

We're responsible, because of our common humanity, for the way we exercise the power money always conveys. That power can take many forms, and can be used to create goodness, to inflict pain, or left unexplored. Power left dormant is opportunity lost.

CHAPTER FIVE

Resolving the Provider/ Organizer Dilemma

THE MOST OBVIOUS PLACE where the power of money gets negotiated on a daily basis is in sorting out the "provider" and "organizer" roles. Using the simplest definition, providers are people who bring in money. In a family setting, that means primary and secondary breadwinners. In a work setting, that means people who are in direct-revenue generating roles, like sales. Organizers do everything else. Typically, they create the conditions under which providers can make the most efficient use of their time. Organizers support, maintain, do background and advance work, crunch numbers, analyze, systematize, track, solve problems, and smooth over conflicts. Organizers are masters at herding cats.

The provider/organizer role dilemma may be the most concrete, and at the same time, the most universal of money's hard questions. Clients of mine whose family income barely meets the $40,000 level have provider/organizer issues. Families who earn $200,000 a year and up have provider/organizer issues. Businesses, nonprofit agencies, health care institutions, governmental bodies, large universities, and public school districts all have tensions around the provider/organizer roles that beg to be identified and resolved.

Why do I call sorting out provider/organizer roles a "dilemma"?

Providers almost always get paid much, much more than organizers. In almost any system – work or family – providers get more recognition, more status, have more influence over outcomes, have a wider range of options, and exercise much more power. Providers' work is very visible, typically hands-on, and very measurable. What was your sales revenue for the year? How much in grants did you bring in? How many new patients did you add? How many full-tuition students have enrolled? How many billable hours did you complete? How many contracts did you close, and what was the net revenue added to the firm?

Organizers almost always get paid less – not because their work is unimportant but because it's much harder to figure out how to value it. Another factor adding to the dilemma is that organizers get a derivative satisfaction from their work; their sense of accomplishment usually comes from making others shine. They often wait months or years – sometimes in futility and frustration – to be recognized, affirmed, and adequately compensated. If an organizer performs superbly, he or she is relatively invisible. Everything "just flows smoothly," or the right information is "just there when it's needed most," or the contract documents are "all in order for the signing," and who's really going to take time to figure out how to compensate or recognize someone for that?

The Impact of the Dilemma

The universe is heavily tilted financially toward providers, in ways both large and small. The financial difference is not always accounted for by a demonstrable variation in the value of the work. That, in a nutshell, is the provider/organizer dilemma. Top litigators at big law firms typically make more than the managing partner. Ordinary money managers who lure profitable clients to investment houses typically make more than brilliant analysts. People who close deals for real estate investment trusts typically make more than managers who maintain and upgrade the properties once they're in the portfolio. Travel agents who sell airline tickets and book vacation packages typically make more than product development staff who locate and assemble the inventory to be sold.

An Internet company holding a day-long meeting at the home office planned to fly in the sales staff from all outlying regional offices so they could continue working on their company-provided laptops while waiting for the others to arrive. Everyone else – client service staff, operations, administrative and secretarial – was brought in by bus.

The impact of the provider/organizer dilemma is wider than "who gets paid what, and why?" The universe is also tilted in terms of the range of things providers and organizers wind up doing. My Iowa aunts and uncles both worked hard on their farms in the 1950s. We visited them in the stifling August heat, when my aunts would wear short-sleeved cotton housedresses and sturdy shoes. I remember their wiry forearms and muscular calves. When haying time came, they were out in the fields with the men, tossing heavy bales into the wagons to get the crop under cover before the late afternoon rains. I never saw my uncles in the kitchen helping with the canning, the preserving, the cleaning, the mending, or the care and feeding of the lambs, calves, and children.

Providers work hard, but they get to focus. Their time is valuable and not to be frittered away on routine matters. Organizers also work hard, but they have to juggle multiple and competing demands. They often have a day that never ends. One of my first adult work experiences was to serve as a Peace Corps volunteer in rural Panama, where I lived about fifteen feet away from a local couple with ten children ages thirteen and under. I vividly recall the early evening hours after a long day of work – every able-bodied adult in the village worked long hours to supply the most basic needs. The husband and primary provider, Roberto, would sit on a bench in front of the house, smoking one of the two cigarettes he bought for a nickel every day, his children tumbling and playing at this feet. His common-law wife, Minga, would get up, hoist the five-gallon can to her head, and set off to fill the water barrel one last time, wash up the bowls and cups from dinner, nurse the babies, and get the rest of the children corralled and into the house for bed. Then she would finally join me in the rocking chairs in front of my house, ready to sit and talk. Little time would pass before Roberto would come around the corner and pointedly announce he was ready for bed. Her eyes would blaze as she watched his retreating back. Defiantly, she would remain seated. "He always wants to be on top, on top, on top."

As you read you may be thinking, "Those examples are of another time, and even another country. Surely with American women now in the work force earning good money, the dynamic you describe is no longer true." Our 1950's and 1960's version of the provider/organizer dilemma was largely gender-specific. Those of us in mid-life remember Ozzie Nelson going out to work, while Harriet tended Ricky and David. Ward Cleaver read the evening paper in his suit, while June got dinner ready in her heels, dress, and pearls. Jacqueline Kennedy organized the White House; JFK ran the country. That sharp gender distinction is no longer true. Many American men now share some responsibility for home and hearth; that can even mean becoming "house-Dads," with primary responsibility for raising the children and supporting their high-powered traveling wives. Even more striking is the shift for women. Those of us in our 40s and 50s are the first generations to be widely in the work force in professional positions, with financial independence in our own right, and with our hands on multiple levels of power. Gay men and lesbians now openly raise their own families and juggle the provider/organizer roles along with typical gender expectations. Single moms and dads both work and raise children. Single men and women without children or long-term companions are faced with the complex challenge of resolving provider/organizer issues within themselves.

The provider/organizer dynamic has, over time, grown more diverse, more complicated, and less-gender specific, yet the core dilemmas still rumble beneath the surface of our lives. We even have, among the $250,000 and up crowd, a replay of the 1950's story. A 2000 *Wall Street Journal* article entitled "The New Economy Family" profiled families where Dad earns so much it doesn't "pay" for Mom to work. Rather than retain their hard-won new gender roles, both men and women seem to lapse back into very traditional patterns. One man found himself thinking, "I'm paying for this" as he and his wife differed over the design for an upgrade to the house. One woman who gave up her $80,000-a-year job as an environmental-issues manager was turned down for a credit card. Her conclusion was: "OK, I'm officially a stay-at-home mom. I have no power in this family or in society."

Variations on the Role Dilemma

On a personal level, we all have a responsibility for seeing to our financial needs, and those of the people we love. We all need a roof over our heads, money for necessities and for crises, money to get an ice cream on the hottest day of the summer, and money to sustain us in our old age. Seeing to those needs falls to the "provider" side of the ledger. We also all have a responsibility, at some deep level of psychological necessity, to create a sense of "home." For most of us, "feeling at home" has to do with a physical place, with our belongings, with food and fragrant smells, with customs and rituals, with the comforting rhythms of daily life. Seeing to those needs falls to the "organizer" side.

On a business level, everyone who's part of an organization has a responsibility to the business model – to know and act in accord with whatever balance between income and outgo allows the company or institution to thrive. That's the "provider" part of a professional setting. People also have a need for things to run smoothly so we can get our work done and achieve a level of accomplishment and self-worth. That's the "organizer" side. My consulting practice has focused on the fast-growth entrepreneurial business market. Company founders who start with one account, a few employees, and a work culture where everyone is "one of the gang" often call me three or four years later in sheer desperation. Suddenly, they find themselves with a multi-million-dollar operating budget, seventy-five to one hundred employees, no consistent systems, and daily chaos. Fixing the problem falls to my teaching the founders to augment the "provider" strengths that have made the company grow with mastery of the "organizer" role. At this point founders, on my strong recommendation, often hire their first CFO. They begin to widen the leadership team beyond the original small group, with managerial skill being newly valued in the people who are promoted and given more responsibility. They establish policies instead of shooting from the hip on operational decisions. They hire someone for HR who knows about compliance and regulatory issues, not just "good-with-people" types who can think up cool recruitment and retention tools like on-site massages, dry cleaning pickup, and extreme sport company retreats.

Some people are intuitively skilled at both providing and organizing. Some of us share providing/organizing roles on a roughly equal basis with a spouse, partner, or colleague. Some of us provide, and outsource the "organizer" role. Some of us organize, and hook up with a provider, making the necessary trade-offs to get the financial security we need. Some of us struggle to do either.

Vera, a professor at a well-recognized medical school, is both a provider and an organizer. She is very talented at getting large grants and in publishing the results of her research. She is equally skilled at mentoring young interns and residents, showing them how to think simultaneously like practitioners and researchers. Her institution has always valued the provider skills – her ability to get grants and extend the visibility of the university in scholarly publications – more highly than her organizer skills of mentoring and faculty committee service. On a personal level, Vera, now in her late 50's, told me, "I've always been professionally ambitious; that's never been a problem. Earlier in my life I thought I would die if I didn't also marry and have children. That didn't happen, and I didn't die. I had to learn how to create a home for myself, and to draw in people I cared about."

The rewards for someone who integrates the provider/organizer roles are twofold: the ability to focus intently on career, and the resiliency that comes from having to develop a broad range of capacities within oneself. The main risk is that the "provider" role may look much easier to tackle, tempting the individual to focus full attention on professional advancement. We live in a very couples-and-family-oriented society; the word "home" connotes "place where one lives with a spouse or partner and children." In truth, "home" means "a sense of feeling at home, safe, at rest" – surely a psychological entitlement longed for by all of us, without exception. For a very results-oriented person, the task of "creating home" can seem unbearably touchy-feely and elusive.

Linda and Ron, a couple in their late 50's, share the provider/organizer roles. Both are long-time public school teachers and now, toward the end of their careers, building-level-administrators. For much of their married life they have worked similar hours and earned similar salaries. Before they could afford cleaning help, they divided household chores roughly equally. She cleaned the upstairs; he did the downstairs. He did the laundry; she did the grocery shopping. Together they raised one son and were very active in his life, supporting fund-raising activities for the high school band, serving as a host family, and as officers in his Operation Friendship travel organization. The rewards have been high. They are both significant figures in their son's life. They have shared professional interests for over thirty years. They continue to spend a great deal of time with each other, working on things they both value. They have accumulated a deep reserve of shared experiences, and were not "strangers" in their relationship when their son left home for college and the need for active parenting grew less intense.

The risk for those who share provider/organizer roles on a roughly equal basis falls most heavily on the professional side. With neither going full out, the career trajectory for both can be affected. Linda and Ron are talented enough to have become public school superintendents, education school faculty members, entrepreneurs in the for-profit management of schools, speakers and writers on the urgent topic of effective education, or Department of Education officials responsible for high-level policy-setting. That did not happen. Instead, they make a difference for children, teachers, staff, and families at the building level – Ron as principal of an elementary school, Linda as vice-principal of a middle school.

Stan has been a traditional sole provider with a stay-at-home wife; he's a successful senior executive in his mid-50's, widely recognized for his intelligence, professional competence, and community leadership. He and his wife Ginny raised two daughters; Ginny also organized the smooth running of the household around Stan's long hours and sometimes heavy travel schedule. She has been at his side for the numerous corporate functions at which their presence as a happily married couple has been important. When Ginny died suddenly, Stan was shocked to find himself – for the first time ever – feeling isolated, profoundly depressed, mentally scattered, and subject to panic attacks. His world had lost its organizing center, and he had never developed the skills to create the feeling of being "at home" or "at rest" on his own. He was also tentative in reaching out to his grieving daughters without Ginny there to guide the interaction.

Anastasia is what I call a "counterculture" sole provider; she, not her husband, is the primary breadwinner for the family. Her husband retired early to care for and raise their two sons while Anastasia climbed the corporate ladder. Now in her early 40's, she is a senior executive, a director of diversity for a global sportswear manufacturer. A Haitian woman, Anastasia comes from a strong tradition of powerful matriarchs. Several years ago, Anastasia fell into a severe clinical depression when she realized she had been on the road traveling for every single childhood milestone her firstborn son had reached.

Now in her 50's, Mary Frances is also a counterculture provider, although her now-deceased husband was not a stay-at-home dad. They utilized day care and summer camps while raising their children, and household help to run their home. Counter to most statistics on black urban professionals, she generated a salary far higher than her husband's. She earned more, and wanted more. At the height of what she describes as "my materialistic mind set," she had committed them to a custom-built 4000 square foot home in a wealthy suburb. While the home was under construction, her then 38-year-old husband suffered his first heart attack. Two weeks before the scheduled closing date, he was diagnosed with potentially fatal cardiovascular disease, and told he needed an immediate heart transplant, which he had no more than a 50/50 chance of surviving. Mary Frances went to the builder and said, "I'm walking"; she and her husband lost $50,000 in penalties. In retrospect, Mary Frances sees her intense upward striving as having unnerved her husband, causing him additional unwelcome stress.

The rewards for providers are many: financial security, power, prestige, and the opportunity to stretch yourself to solve challenging business problems, among others. The risks are heavy on both the personal and professional side. Personally, providers may fail to develop sufficient skills around creating intimacy, relying instead on others – usually their spouses or partners – to mediate relationships for them. When that mediating person is no longer available, the provider can feel shockingly lost. Also, high-achieving providers may devote most waking hours to their work, leaving little of themselves for relationships. I once spoke with the owner of a small manufacturing firm who was lamenting the fact that his grown daughters had moved out and moved on, and now had little time for him. He felt they had come and gone in his life, and he barely knew them. I could hear the sadness in his voice, and asked if he had taken any steps to change the expectations within his company so that younger mothers and fathers would not feel that they had to absent themselves from family life in order to climb the ladder of success. He glared at me in silence. If you want something about your money story to be different, you have to act differently. Merely lamenting what you've lost doesn't do much.

On the professional side, providers run a risk that I call "living by the sword means you'll probably die by the sword." The culture of success values running with the pack, preferably at the head of the pack. There is little tolerance for the turbulence and distraction that may come from personal illness, exhaustion, family crisis, missing the mark on a job assignment, falling out of favor with the person to whom you report, falling behind in adding new skills, or difficulty keeping up with current technologies. As colleagues fall by the wayside, you probably find you don't have the time or inclination to look back, thinking their bad fortune to be a function of some weakness on their part. If you fall by the wayside, no one among your colleagues is likely to stop and help you get back on track either. When you're off their radar screen, you're gone. "Get back with the pack on your own if you can" is likely to be the message.

June Cleaver's Revenge

June Cleaver and her 1950's television sisters were the model organizers for women of my generation. June's home was always neat; her children had mild differences but never got really down and dirty with each other; and, most of all, she put a hot homemade dinner on the table every single night. Her young children would never, as mine once did, proclaim "the Highland Park diner" as their favorite home-cooked meal.

Most of us who worked and did the primary child rearing and household organizing – often with paid services of many kinds – did not live up to our TV role models. Nor did we have many real-life role models. Our own mothers mostly stayed at home, or worked in low-paying jobs in factories, luncheonettes, or department stores. Some women "went to business"; often they wore quasi-masculine attire and were childless. Some women, like my mother, had to return to work because their husbands fell ill or died, and they weren't happy about it. Mary Frances and I and other mid-life women tried to do it all. We chose to work, and got demanding jobs. We wanted to have children, and be primary figures in raising them. We wanted marriages that had a life of their own, not just an identity as "parents." We didn't want live-in help, because we were stretched so thin emotionally we couldn't imagine having to incorporate someone else into our households. We somehow cobbled marriage, career and family together, all the while worrying about the impact on our kids. Mary Frances sees the effects on her son and daughter as the price paid for her own superwoman years. "I missed a lot of their growing up. While they've both turned out well, I missed a lot of bonding. That idea of 'quality time' is bull. You can only get quality if you give quantity, and I didn't. When my daughter was ten, a friend took me aside and told me I had to spend more time being my daughter's mom."

When my own children were about ten and twelve, I was nearly undone by what we now remember humorously as "June Cleaver's revenge." Preparing to leave the house for an early evening meeting, I was overwhelmed with guilt that my children and husband were planning to eat grilled cheese sandwiches. With five minutes to spare before being on my way, dressed in a suit and heels, I retrieved a large block of frozen chicken and a bag of broccoli from the freezer, and began to bang around the kitchen with pots, lids, and table settings. Matt wandered into the kitchen, watched wide-eyed for a few moments, and then asked what in the world I was doing.

"I'm fixing you chicken and broccoli for your dinner. June Cleaver never fed her children grilled cheese." My voice, high and taut, was just shy of the frequency needed to shatter glass.

Matt and Sara had seen "Leave It to Beaver" on cable. Seeming to know what I meant, Matt asked, "But, Mom, did you want to be a June Cleaver kind of mother?" As his question stopped me cold, Matt went on to explain. "We want grilled cheese for dinner. Dad and I and Sara worked it out before school. We don't want dinner to take a long time because afterwards Dad and I are going to play catch while Sara rides her bike with Dana. Then we're doing our homework, and then we're watching the game on TV together until you come home. It's fine, Mom. You can go to your meeting." Following the wisdom of my ten-year-old son, I did.

Many of us now in mid-life were trying to sidestep the immense risk we had seen the traditional organizers – women the ages of our mothers and grandmothers – take. In our eyes the risk was both financial and psychological, and carried a potentially heavier price than we wanted to pay.

Judith has been a traditional organizer, and is now a woman who grapples with the fallout from that role. Currently in her early 70's, Judith is the wife of a retired university president. She grew up in California, the daughter of struggling citrus farmers. Financial anxiety was constant part of daily life during those years – for Judith, for her shy, reserved father, and especially for her anxious and distracted mother. Judith went to Holy Names College in Oakland, then, at the insistence of her parents, transferred to Berkeley and then to UCLA. She wanted to be a journalist, but found few newspaper jobs open to women in San Francisco and the competition fierce. She met her husband, a rising young academic, and gladly allowed him to take the role of provider. "There wasn't anything I was just dying to do, and my husband was very clear about his career path. We talked about my staying at home with our children, and that's what I did."

I asked Judith if she had been aware at the time of the financial risk she was taking. "I didn't really think about it, although I think I realized it. When you're young you think your marriage will work out. In the worst case, I always assumed my husband would support us anyway, even if we were no longer married."

Judith's marriage did work out, although as a shy person like her father she struggled mightily with the public role of wife of the university president. She recalls making a trip with her husband to visit an elderly couple from whom the university expected a large bequest, remembering that the performance anxiety of the weekend "made me almost nauseous."

Judith is clear about the rewards of her life as a wife, mother, and public figure. She and her husband have a decades-long marriage. They have raised three children, and have a wonderful grandchild. They are financially secure; the economic anxiety of Judith's early life can finally be set to rest. During their active academic life, Judith got to travel widely and to meet important intellectuals, artists, and authors. She met a constant stream of famous people coming and going through the university, often having the chance to entertain them at the president's house.

Judith is also very clear about the cost to her sense of self:

> I was squelched. I just felt held in. It was terrible. You learned to play roles. I kept some sense of myself during those years, but to this day I'm not always sure of my voice. My tongue felt tied. The feminist movement really kicked things off for me. I met a circle of Christian feminist theologians and writers. They taught me that to be a woman, I had to tell a woman's story.

These days, with many fewer public commitments and time to explore her own interests, Judith has found her voice. She's hard at work writing her memoir. She has had some short essays published. She has done a public reading of a piece she wrote honoring an important educator in her life at Holy Names College. Judith's one hope is that she retains her faculties and physical energy long enough to write down everything she needs to say.

Paulina is in her mid-80's, a homemaker, a wife, mother of two grown sons, a grandmother, and a good daughter to her own mother, for whom she faithfully cared until her death at 102. Praised for her selflessness in these traditional roles, this sturdy, white-haired woman shook her head in anger and frustration. "All my life I've taken care of others. Here I am an old woman, and I've never had a life of my own." On her mother's death, Paulina received a small cash legacy and the title to her mother's modest home. This is the first time in eight decades Paulina has owned financial assets in her own name.

Organizers in family systems who lack current job skills or some other way to provide for themselves and their children, such as the income from an inheritance, run an immense financial risk. They are subject to making do with what a provider is willing or able to give them, and that dependence can profoundly distort the power balance in their relationships. Organizers in the workplace also run a financial risk. The work they do simply makes things run right. Bosses find it hard to locate an external reference point to help determine how to value organizing work relative to the overall business model. In addition to the financial risk, people who focus on organizing home or workplace run a huge psychological risk. Because the role is most often supportive and reactive, it can be hard for organizers to be initiators, even when the issue at hand falls squarely into their area of expertise. Finally, being so keyed into the needs of others often makes it hard for organizers to be strong advocates for their own needs and expectations.

There are people who struggle to do either provider or organizer well. Joel has two grown sons, both in their early 30's, well- educated, intelligent, and personable. One son is what Joel calls "settled." The man is married, working at a good job, and has given Joel and his wife two grandchildren. The other son struggles personally and professionally, moves in and out of jobs and relationships, and is what Joel sees as "tremendously dependent." Joel has never let his son fail. Joel recognizes that he may have done his son more harm than good, and that the use of money to bail a grown man out over and over again has been negative. Joel's wife has disagreed with him on the treatment of their son, but allows Joel's wishes to prevail. "She knows how intensely I feel, how upset I get, when our son has problems." Joel has no illusions about the relative success of his efforts to smooth out his son's troubled life:

> I was told ten years ago by a psychologist that if I didn't let go and let my son fail or succeed on his own, I would be doing the same things ten

years hence that I was doing then. I ignored the advice, and the psychologist was absolutely right. Now I don't know how to get off the
trapeze. I simply don't know how to get off. My son isn't well. He struggles continually with depression – not serious, but ongoing. He's terribly
unhappy with his life. I feel sorry, and try to make it up with money and
power. It isn't the best way, but I don't know the best way. In a sense my
son is an accomplice to my behavior. He enjoys the part of my intervening in his life that he enjoys, and is angry about the part he doesn't.

Joel is an intelligent and successful man, with a keen insight into his
own actions and those of his son. Joel is also what psychologists sometimes refer to as "stuck" in a behavior pattern that shows no signs of
a good outcome. Interestingly enough, remaining stuck in ineffective
behaviors is something Joel rarely did in his professional life, where
he was much more demanding of himself and others. To change such
a deeply embedded pattern, Joel is likely to need professional help,
something difficult for a decisive and hard-charging former CEO to
acknowledge. The goal of therapeutic support would not be to "fix"
the younger man, but to guide Joel in learning to respond to his son
as an adult, not as a needy child.

How Times Have Changed

Provider/organizer dilemmas have become more diverse, more complicated, and less gender-specific. Young women get to be job-
focused, ambitious, and financially hungry; young men get to long
for babies way before the women in their lives are ready to consider
being tied down. The key elements of the provider/organizer
dilemma remain: How do we value relative contributions? How do we
make room for people to develop multiple sides of themselves? How
do we teach both men and women to protect themselves against
undue risk – financial, psychological, or both? How well do we care
for kids in our busy and fragmented lives?

    Isabel is 22 and grew up in an apartment on the Upper East Side
of Manhattan, where having a doorman was "the norm." She is now
working as a legal assistant for a large corporate law firm and plans

to attend law school. She anticipates three grueling years of study, followed by the equally demanding five- to seven-year associate path to partnership, then, as a partner, having to meet a billable hour requirement of 1900 hours a year while bringing in profitable new clients. She wonders how children will fit in. She wonders about finding the right young man to marry.

> There are guys in my group of friends who definitely expect that Mom will be at home packing the kids' lunches and that when they come home from work at night dinner will be on the table. These guys are clueless. They have expectations of what they want their lives to be like, and what they expect of their family and their wives, but they have no idea what their wives might be doing other than raising their kids.

Money scares Isabel to death. This job is the first time she has actually earned money. Previously, her parents provided her with money for school and money to spend. She began work with very little idea of budgeting, of paying bills, of saving or investing, but she is bright and her skill level has grown. She earns $40,000 a year, which allows her to manage "fine" on a day-to-day basis, although she is not saving or investing as much as she would like. Much of the work she is asked to do is similar to the work given to first- and second-year associates, people who already have their law degrees and who make two to three times what legal assistants like Isabel make. I ask if she thinks that's fair. She does. "I think there are rules of the game. If you want to play this game, you play by those rules. You can think the rules are unfair, but this law firm takes kids from the best law schools. You don't necessarily learn in law school all the things you need to know to practice law. You learn by working with partners and upper-level associates and by not succeeding and trying again and not succeeding. You learn to take the criticism and persevere. You make more as you work your way up. Those are the rules of the game, and I'm not sure they're things I'd be willing to change."

Professionally, Isabel has the goal of making a big difference in the world. At this point in her career, she is undecided whether that means a law practice in a major firm like the one she works in now, or some sort of public policy role. Some of the corporate behavior she sees her law firm defending is not to her liking. At the same time, she recognizes the pay difference between top corporate lawyers and people who work in the public sector, shaping policy.

> It's completely frustrating and I haven't figured it out yet. I have a standard of living that I want to achieve and a certain amount of passion that I want to bring to my job. Somehow I'd like to balance those two out. I'm hoping that somewhere along the way I'll find that perfect job that will fit in the middle. There are days when I can really see how some of these attorneys have a very comfortable living and provide their families with a comfortable living – and they never get to see their families because of all the hours they have to bill. I don't know if I can deal with that. I want to find something that I love and where I can make money. It has to be possible. It has to be out there somewhere. At least, I hope it is.

In terms of finding a potential marriage partner, Isabel sounds more certain of her expectations. "I find ambition so attractive, and I detest non-ambitiousness. I love people who have goals and go out there and achieve them. I like the fighters and passionate people of the world. I don't like slackers, and I don't like the attitude that 'somebody else will do it.' It's going to be really hard for me to end up with someone who isn't as ambitious or even more ambitious than I am. I think we would be splitting child care right down the line. I don't necessarily like the idea of a nanny raising my kids, but I spent a whole lot of time with babysitters, and we had a nanny too. I'm not willing to be a full-time mom for very long, so I think I'd want child care evenly split."

Isabel seems headed for a model that I call "provider/provider, with organizer largely outsourced." Her future can be described by what is commonly thought of as "power couple." The rewards of this model can be substantial in terms of financial security, social power, professional prestige, and self-esteem. The risks are also substantial. On the business side, two ambitious spouses can become killer competitive with each other. On the personal side, there is often little "hanging-out time" for either the couple or for the children of such a marriage. These are the kids who grow up in organized and supervised activities for most of their waking hours to keep them safely occupied, and to satisfy their parents' longing for high-achieving off-spring.

Ben is 27, a Web designer and soon to be married to the young woman he's been with for the last five years. Ben is ready to have a baby; his fianceé – a freelance photographer with three or four years of school ahead of her – is not.

> I tease her about a wedding night conception, but I'm not really serious. I think we're on totally the same page – I'm just more in a baby mode. I see babies and I think, "I want one of those." She sees babies and she tells me, "Not for a few years – let's keep walking."

Ben's readiness for parenthood has to do, in large measure, with the early death of his own father. "My Dad passed away while I was a junior in college. He was only 48. Part of it probably comes from wanting to be in my children's lives for as many years as possible; the earlier I have kids, the more years they're going to have of me. Part of feeling ready also probably has to do with never feeling a generation gap between my parents and myself. I never had a problem relating to them, and I think it's because we weren't that far apart in age. I have a friend who's my age and his Dad is in his 70's. They hardly talk."

Ben was close to both of his parents, although they divorced when he was in the fifth grade. He lived with his Mom five days a week, and with his Dad the other two. The feeling about money was relaxed while his parents were together; neither was very materialistic, and they valued education for Ben above most other things. After the split, money matters became more fraught with anxiety, because there were now two households to support on two modest incomes. Ben remembers being aware of the anxiety, but not feeling drawn into it. "My parents were great about not involving me in their own issues. They had stuff to deal with, but they kept me out of it. I never had to worry about money."

Ben's most painful experience with money came after his father's death.

> I got $90,000 in life insurance; I was 20 years old. I gave Mom $30,000, so I had $60,000 left. The money was from my Dad dying. I spent it in a

year, every penny, and then I couldn't stop so I got credit cards and spent money on those. I didn't want the money. It felt like blood money. I knew on some level I was depressed and I thought the toys would make me feel better – but a little while after I had bought something I'd go back to feeling screwed again. People say that if I had kept the money and invested it, I'd be doing well today. I look at what I did with the money. I bought a recording studio and I recorded and released three CDs that were largely about the experience of losing my father. Those were real healing steps. That all cost a lot of money, but I could have sat in therapy for a year and not have begun to heal in the way I did from making these recordings.

The personal debt that Ben is still working through leads him and his fianceé to keep very separate finances, at Ben's insistence. They deposit the same amount of money in a joint account each month, and from there they pay shared expenses. Ben is adamant about the responsibility for his consumer debt remaining with him. At the same time, he envisions sharing child care when he and his fianceé start a family. He's willing to take the possible negative consequences to his career. "I didn't grow up in a household where getting somewhere on a professional level was a priority. My parents placed priority on get-ting somewhere as a person. When I was looking at colleges, my Dad took me aside and told me not to ever get lost in credentials. He said your title and where you went to school don't matter – what matters is what you do with it. Here's guy who went to Haverford, then to Oxford in England for his M.A., then to UPenn for his Ph.D.; and he's telling me what kind of person you are matters more than what credentials you amass. That was eye-opening."

Ben and his fianceé seem headed for a model similar to that of Linda and Ron: "provider/organizer and provider/organizer, with some outside help." The biggest rewards of this model have to do with what kind of people parents and children can become, both individ-ually and as a family unit. The risks, of which Ben is well aware, are professional. He may make less of a footprint on the world as a Web designer than could be the case if he focused more heavily on his pro-fession; his footprint will have to do with the kind of creative artist, husband, and father he will become.

Where Are You Now?

This chapter has offered several models through which you can address provider/organizer issues. Each model has both rewards and risks. The following questions will help you determine which model comes closest to what you're doing now, and to what you aspire to do in the future. The questions will also point you toward other possible models as you consider alternatives to your current provider/organizer role definition. As you read the questions, do a "forced choice" among the five. Although you may be attracted to elements of more than one model, push yourself to say which one most closely describes where you are now. Then ask yourself which one most closely describes where you would like to be. Take time to carefully consider the trade-offs inherent in each model.

> *How much do you value ambition as the driving force for you own professional life, and for that of your partner or spouse?*

If you're here, or aspire to be here in the future, you've chosen the model I call "provider/provider, with organizer largely outsourced." You'll probably make a lot of money, and get a lot of professional recognition and rewards. On the personal side, this model can leave very little room for interpersonal development or for kids. On the business side of the relationship, spouses can easily carry the killer competitive work style over to their marriage. If you choose this model, be mindful of the cost. If the cost is falling most heavily on your marriage and on your kids, is that what you want?

> *How strongly do you feel about neither partner or spouse supporting the other, but both supporting the family unit plus having time to be deeply involved with each other and with children?*

This choice is what I refer to as "provider/organizer and provider/ organizer, with some outside help." This model may have a large effect on the career trajectory for both, since neither is going full-out to climb a career ladder. The model can be annoying for employers whose commitment to "work/life balance" may be defined as "as long as it doesn't involve key people in my department." Big upsides are possible with this model in terms of individual and family growth. If you choose this option, you have to be dead honest with yourself about the level of your ambition – about what level of professional success is "enough" for you to feel satisfied.

How deeply does building your personal and professional life around traditional role definitions contribute to your sense of meaning and order in the world?

If this is important to you, you've probably chosen "traditional provider/organizer" as your model. In this case, the male provides financially for the family unit and makes most financial decisions. The female stays at home and organizes the children, the family's social life, and volunteer commitments. This model creates a big psychological risk for the provider and his ability to create "home," should that ever be necessary, and a big financial risk for the organizer. When it works, the rewards can be financial security for all, an orderly office and home life, Mom as the model for family values instead of a sitter, and a hot meal on the table at night. If you choose this model, is there any way you can compensate for the lopsided risks? Can you put more financial assets in the organizer's name – and not claim them back again in the event of a divorce? If you're the provider, can you make a commitment to form at least one deep relationship that isn't with a "work friend," just so you learn how to do it? If you're an organizer at work, you have a big challenge: defining the worth of what you do and negotiating to get paid for it. You can't rely on whatever system you work in to do that for you.

How important is it for you to be who you really are, whether or not that fits with traditional role definitions and societal norms?

If you're here, you may well have chosen the "counterculture provider/organizer." One example is female as provider and male as organizer. Males may then be "outsiders" to most of their peers, which may have a significant impact on the male ego and on the marriage over the long term. Females may be highly successful professionally, and highly vulnerable to sudden attacks of "June Cleaver's revenge." Another example is gay and lesbian couples – still deemed counterculture within American society – who have to juggle established gender role models along with their own negotiated balance of provider/organizer. Can a gay man choose to be an organizer of home and hearth without reprising Nathan Lane's brilliant diva role in *Birdcage*? Can an ambitious lesbian provider be accepted as feminine, and not be dismissed as a man-hater behind her back? If you choose a counterculture model, can you find a supportive community that will help you work through the issues and not leave you feeling so isolated and vulnerable?

How important is it for you to focus on your own creative passions, beliefs, and personal pathways, without wanting to make the kinds of accommodations that often come with a sustained commitment to one other person?

This choice describes what I call "internal provider/organizer," with both roles integrated within the same person. The main risk here is that individual will overidentify with whichever role feels easier, and fail to develop the skills to handle the other side of the ledger. This model can be highly rewarding developmentally in terms of the ability to focus on one's own vision and commitments, without having to bend very much to the needs and rhythms of others. Again, if you choose this model, be sure you have a community of like-minded people with whom you can explore and resolve major issues that arise.

Our relationship with money creates specific societal roles that I refer to as "provider" and "organizer." Providers bring in money directly; organizers earn money indirectly by supporting the efforts of providers. Making that role relationship intentional, and assuming responsibility for the risks and rewards of the model we choose, are essential aspects of a mature money story.

CHAPTER SIX

"What's Money For:
Me, or We?"

IF YOU SPEND FIFTY OR SIXTY or more hours a week on activities that generate money, toward what end are you doing it? Close in complexity to "how do you wield money's power?" and "how do you resolve the provider/organizer dilemma?" comes this question: "what's money for?" I have a bias – or personal conviction – on this one, which I will tell you at the outset: if you want to make a really big footprint on the world, you have to consider something bigger in scope than your own foot. That means money has to be as much about "we" as it is about "me." Who, you might wonder, are the "we"?

Minga, whom you met briefly in the last chapter, is in her early 60's if she is still living. I first met her in 1967, when I was 22 and newly assigned to my Peace Corps site in rural Panama. Minga was my landlady. She, her common-law husband Roberto, and their ten surviving children lived in a truly tiny mud and tin house just behind mine. My two-room house was merely small. For twice as much space as they had, a concrete instead of a dirt floor, and a shared outhouse, my monthly rent was five dollars. Minga – whose roles included wife, mother, coprovider for her family, household organizer, and community leader – was then 29.

With access to any real money, Minga could easily have been a power broker of the caliber of Josh, Art, and Katherine. Like Josh, she was highly entrepreneurial. The Panamanian government ran a daily national lottery; the tickets cost a dollar. That amount was far out of reach for anyone in our village of Rio Hato, so Minga devised her own knockoff version at five cents a ticket. Late in the morning, after she had built a fire to make coffee, bought bread at the local tienda for everyone's breakfast, nursed the newborn and the two-year-old, packed Roberto some bread and mangoes to take to the fields for his lunch, gotten everyone dressed and the older children off to school, carried water from the well to wash everyone's clothes, done the washing by hand and hung it to dry, nursed the babies again, and made thin watery soup with yucca for the younger children's lunch, she left the babies in the care of their slightly older siblings and set off to sell her chances. On any given day, she'd collect twenty or thirty nickels from our village of 200 or so families. The radio would announce the winning numbers in the late afternoon, and she and the winner would split the pot. Roberto brought home about $1.50 a day from his work in the sugar cane fields; her 50 cents or so brought them up around the $2 range.

The World Bank estimates that over 2.8 billion people live on less than $2 a day. More than 30 years after I first met them, Minga and Roberto live vividly in my memory, giving a human contour to that statistic. They, their children, the rest of the 2.8 billion, and the people living less than a mile from you who haven't yet found their way into the economic system are the "we."

Like Art, Minga was a dealmaker of great finesse. She had been among a small group of villagers that had petitioned for a Peace Corps volunteer to be assigned to serve their community. Now that I had been assigned there, she intended to make the most of the opportunity. From the outset, she was instrumental in plotting how to get others involved in the small cooperative we formed, in picking our focus (buying a cow a week from the local farmers at fair prices, and selling the meat to local villagers at fair prices), and in getting the provincial agent from the Ministry of Agriculture to send resources our way. Like Art, Minga had her own "golden Rolodex" of people on whom she could call, only the names were all in her head.

Minga could, like Katherine, move with blunt force when necessary. When spirits sagged, Minga could always reignite the group's
passion to stand up and swing for the bleachers. "For the children,"
this tiny woman would challenge, with her dark eyes flashing and her
voice hard," we're doing this for our children. Do we want them to
have no more than we have had in our lives?"

I call Minga an entrepreneur, a deal maker, and a mover and
shaker of systems. I hesitate to call her a power broker, because of the
absence of money in the equation. Minga and I eventually gathered
around thirty people to be members of the cooperative; the entry fee
was a dollar, and most had to pay it over time. What we found is that
the power that comes from money, in and of itself, can draw certain
lines in the sand. The power that comes from the labor and shared
hopes of poor people, more likely than not, will be eventually worn
down and run over unless it can become mainstream and attract
money.

That we could not do. We swung big and fell way short. Most of
us got something out of the experience of working together for two
years, but the goal of giving villagers a sustainable leg up on their
everyday grinding poverty was not met.

Parallels Between Now and Then

In many aspects, other than money, the power story of the cooperative of Rio Hato was similar to Josh's company, Art's financial institution, or Katherine's college.

*The role of "leader" was something everyone grew into over time, and shaped
to fit variations in temperaments and abilities.* When I first began to work
with the group, one of our chief assets was that I was young, white,
female, North American, and a Peace Corps volunteer. All of that held
the allure of "difference"; I could easily call the Panamanian Ministry
of Agriculture and get through to someone, even in the early days
when I could hardly speak decent Spanish. The villagers could not get
through, their calls were routinely ignored. Near the end of my two-
year stay, Rufino, the co-op's president, called the main Ministry office

in Panama City and asked respectfully, but insistently, to speak to the minister himself. Rufino, normally a shy and reticent man, persuaded the minister to drive three hours into the countryside with some of his aides to meet with our group and hear about our problems with the people trying to put us out of business. In contrast to the point where the group began, Rufino's rise to fill the position of leader – with the backing and support of the others – was stunning.

The power stories of group members began taking form at a very early age. Public education in rural Panama was at that time free only through the third grade; most of the co-op members were barely literate. Their work choices were slim. Girls usually became pregnant right around puberty – not because they wouldn't have used birth control, but because none was available at a cost they could afford. With many children to raise, young women had to have an extra amount of ambition to do anything outside home and hearth. Minga did her lottery knockoff. Señora Cuta had a roadside stand at which she sold freshly pressed fruit juices and warm sodas – no electricity meant no ice. Some of the local Ministry of Agriculture agents were women. They were the exceptions. Boys were raised to be fishermen, or subsistence farmers tending small plots of sugar cane. A very few made it through high school and became teachers or agriculture agents. They, too, were the exceptions. The story of what a young girl or boy growing up in Rio Hato could aspire to ran something like this: "You can have a family, a roof over your head, enough to eat to keep everyone alive and functioning. You can have a few possessions, like a good machete and a radio. Don't even think you have the power to get more; if you do think that way, your life will be too disappointing."

I was very young and inexperienced back then; I only had a glimmering of how extraordinary it was that some of them did hope, did aspire to write a new story for themselves, their children, and their village.

Financial power in Panamanian culture carried a hard edge. The reason the co-op decided to sell meat had mostly to do with cheating, and a little with wanting some variation on the staple diet of rice and beans. Some of our villagers, and some from outlying villages, had single cows that they had raised and fed through grazing. When the mature cow was sold, they would buy and raise a young calf, pocketing a little extra money in the transaction. The market for cows and the sale of meat throughout the province was entirely locked up by the cousin of the powerful provincial governor. Villagers who brought their cows to be weighed and sold routinely found the animals "short weighted," and their proceeds smaller than should have been the case. In deciding to compete directly with this corrupt system, we were demanding entry into a very rough marketplace.

There is a price to pay for exercising power. We did pay the price, although not right away. For about a year after getting the co-op up and running, we had a string of successes. As word spread around the countryside that we bought fairly, almost every farmer who had a cow committed it to us, sometimes being willing to wait months until we could buy a particular animal for the weekly slaughter. Even with the decision to pay fair prices, the co-op made some money. We started a second project, a community garden that grew produce to be sold in the provincial capital and for which we bought tools beyond their bare hands and machetes. What had fallen off the vines and couldn't be sold, the frugal co-op members took home to their families and ate – even though, initially, eating any vegetable at all was about as appealing as eating grass. As the co-op began to make money and the members began to walk taller in the village, others joined and the membership grew.

Then the hammer came down. After harassment and vague threats from our frustrated competitors failed to persuade us to shut down, we received an explicit threat. If we didn't end our cattle business, some highly visible member of the co-op would disappear.

Not long after I had arrived in Rio Hato at the outset of my tour of service, Panama suffered a military coup. An army general deposed the elected president, Arnulfo Arias, and took over the job of running the country. At that time a man in our village, known to be politically connected with the Arias party, had disappeared. He never returned – nor did anyone go and ask about him, which would have been far too dangerous.

The threat of someone disappearing again was real and terrifying, and set off a bitter debate within the co-op. A few members wanted to continue fighting at all costs; many remained silent or stopped coming to meetings. Others declared, in sad and defeated voices, that we had to stop. After much thought, I agreed that we had to end the cattle operation at least. After more heated discussion and argument, that consensus prevailed. The decision felt right to most of us, but not good.

Within days, the co-op dissolved in rancor. If we couldn't provide meat for the community, the members didn't want to do anything. They were mad at each other, at me, at the minister's empty words, at the thieving politicians, and at el Dios, who had again let them down. This crisis came to a head within a few weeks of the end of my tour of service; the Peace Corps office in Panama City decided not to replace me in the village. In addition to the pain of losing the project, the co-op members felt abandoned.

I'd like to think the good experiences of the two years eventually re-surfaced, allowing the villagers to try swinging for the bleachers again at some later time. I'm not sure that happened, or could have happened given the overwhelming nature of the factors that kept people in poverty: poor education, inadequate nutrition, little medical care beyond natural healers, a legal system that offered no protection for the rights of the poor, upper-class disdain for the "lazy and irresponsible" rural farmer, or *campesino*. My innate skepticism took over, and I never returned to Rio Hato to find out how they fared.

Did the co-op members gain enough benefit, given the amount of sweat equity and hope they had invested in the fight to better their lives? I'm not sure. They could claim some tangible rewards: a little extra money, some tools, a briefly better diet. In return for helping me improve my Spanish, I taught some of them basic English. By the time I left the village, they knew enough words and phrases to have left our rural village to go into what was then the American-run Canal Zone and get jobs as cleaners on one of the military bases, housekeepers for a Panama Canal worker, or busboys at the legendary Tivoli Hotel – surely a mixed reward. They also got intangible benefits while the co-op existed: pride, the experience of running something, the sense that they were in control and had choices in life. In the end, they had to give up most of the intangibles.

What remained for some of us were the relationships. Those were forged through the long evenings at dusk when we smoked and told stories; through the sweltering work of digging a half-acre garden plot with hand tools; through the ritual surrounding the death of village elder Juan Jaramillo; through the sweaty sensuality of rum-soaked outdoor dances; through sharing our nightly rice and beans; through providing the community with meat for as long as we could. The night before I left the village, the core members of the co-op and I had supper together – a live chicken killed just for the event and thrown in the pot with the rice – and said our good-byes. I gave Minga everything I had in my house that didn't belong to the Peace Corps: a table, some chairs, the hammock I slept in, the mosquito net under which I remained all night to keep away malaria-infected bugs. I hid some money – she would accept food that I bought, and clothing for the children, but never money – near the cooking fire where I knew she would find it. The next day I went farther inland to say good-bye to my Peace Corps friends, stayed overnight, then traveled back down the road through Rio Hato on my way to Panama City and to the airport.

As the old Volkswagon bus jammed with people, live chickens, dead iguanas, sacks of rice and oddly-shaped parcels careened through the village, I caught sight of Minga standing alone by the side of the road, in the broiling sun and with all the morning's work to do, peering intently into each passing bus, waiting to catch my eye one more time and say good-bye.

Fast Forward

Here we are, in today's culture of success, both elated and nervous about our hard-earned money. Rising markets make us feel smart and rich. Falling markets cause anxiety and make us feel "poor," but most of us reading this book aren't really poor, no matter how you cut it. Minga and Roberto supported their ten children on about two dollars a day. That's poor. When I went to take possession of my new Jaguar – whose final cost after a trade-in, some haggling, a few extras, and New York state sales tax was in the neighborhood of $50,000 – I simply wrote a check. That's what publications like *The Economist* mean when they talk about the global chasm between "have" and "have-not."

The word "charity," as a way of bridging that chasm, has become dated and fallen out of favor. Those of us who see our money as having a broader social purpose are attracted to the phrase "venture philanthropy" instead. We look to share not only our financial resources, but also our values and skills with nonprofits working for social transformation. Therein lies a dilemma. The very qualities that make us good at getting money in the first place – a laser-like ability to focus, a need for control, a driving ambition – make us terribly impatient at letting other people take the time they need to find their way. That's especially true when our money funds aspects of the often-messy process of upward mobility. We think it's inefficient for people to wander in the economic wilderness, trying to figure out what we've so amply demonstrated. We want to share what we've learned and have them take advantage of the leg up. Then, in our view, everybody wins.

I'm afraid I would be a far less patient Peace Corps volunteer today than I was in 1967. The Peace Corps has always had one core insight that's right on target: the understanding that if people want something about their lives to be different, they have to be the ones to say what "different" means. After going through Peace Corps training, I would never have presumed I knew better than Minga, Roberto, Rufino, and the others what the people of Rio Hato needed in order to get on their economic feet. Today, although my life moves at a much faster pace and I'd struggle to abide by that belief, I still hold it to be true.

Economic models for developing countries are difficult to translate very literally to our far more complex economy. My belief is that the core insight does translate, ringing true both there and here: people – even poor people – get to decide for themselves what "better" means.

These days, successful people have varying approaches and beliefs when it comes to using our money to help make "better" happen – if we do so at all. We also differ on how using money to benefit others can give our own lives a larger sense of meaning.

Jane is in her early 30's, single, savvy, and perennially pumped. She has a good MBA from Northwestern, and a successful track record in operations and supply chain management. Jane comes from a family with a tradition of charitable giving; her mother "probably gives away more than she lives on in a year." For Jane, money is a very tangible measure of her own skill, talent, and persistence. In that, money for Jane is unambiguously "for me." She does give time and energy to philanthropic organizations, but usually not money; she doesn't have a high level of confidence in how nonprofits put money to use.

Sue is also in her early 30's, with a stellar education and enviable work background. She lives in Chicago and works for the e-commerce division of a Los Angeles media conglomerate, traveling there for at least three days of each week. She earns a solid six-figure income, with a package of benefits and perks that tries to alleviate the stress of constant travel. She does have a sense of wanting to give back financially, but little time to sort out one philanthropic opportunity from another. She sometimes makes donations to organizations in the place where she grew up, since she retains some sense of what they actually do.

Lourdes is in her early 60's, and a devout Catholic. For her, money clearly has a larger purpose of social justice, honoring what her church calls "a preferential option for the poor." She deliberately gives time and financial support to organizations that serve marginalized people. Her husband brought in a secure income as head of a research lab for a Fortune 500 company, leaving Lourdes free to devote her professional life to low-paying but spiritually satisfying church work.

Dr. Muhammad Yunus is in his early 50's, a Bangladeshi academic known as "banker to the poor." Yunus is founder of the Grameen Bank, a microlending institution that currently lends more than $1.5 million a day to the poor of Bangladesh. The venture is unique in that it's a for-profit endeavor that risks putting money and control directly into the hands of poor borrowers, giving them the same chance everyone else has to figure out upward mobility. In 1976, seeking to make academia more relevant to the life of the world, Yunus, then head of the economics department at Chittagong University, visited a nearby village. Struck by the villagers' need, he lent $27 from his own pocket to forty-two stool makers to purchase the raw materials for their trade. From there, the Grameen experiment grew to its present form.

What's Your Money For?

If you're working fifty or sixty hours a week and steadily building assets, what's the money for? Is it primarily for "me," or can it also be about "we"? "We" can mean something on a grand and global scale, like Grameen. "We" can also mean extended family, local community, or one's chosen kindred spirits.

Each of the people profiled thus far has responded differently to the question of "me" or "we." Each is successful by current social and economic standards. None is a "greedy Gordon Gecko," a Wall Street barbarian who wields money with blatant disregard for others. Their choices about money give rise to questions that will help you clarify where you see yourself:

Do I pretty much believe "money is for me," but do other things to keep myself aware that I'm part of a larger whole?

Do I try to act on a belief that "money is partly for we," but find it hard to accomplish intelligently when I'm so busy?

Do I live according to the belief that sharing my time, talent, and money is a stewardship commitment, an act of religious faith?

Do I believe that using money to attack the systems of poverty is an inescapable part of living in a global community?

Which statement comes closest to explaining what purpose money serves in your life? If none of these fit, how would you describe what you think making money is for?

Money can basically be used in four ways: money can be "created . . . consumed . . . hoarded . . . distributed." Jane, who believes

in "money for me," is a creator. She uses money as a tangible scorecard to measure her own success. She works as hard as necessary to
generate enough money to keep her scorecard competitive. She also
plays hard. Because she makes a lot of money when she is working,
Jane has no hesitation about giving herself months-long sabbaticals
to remain out of the work force and travel with a backpack to places
like Guatemala, where she seeks out experiences that take her
beyond "conventional tourist."

Neither Jane nor Sue nor Lourdes are great consumers. We don't
have to look far to find people who are. When I started college in
1963, I carried a radio, a blue Royal portable typewriter, and a couple of suitcases of clothes. When my daughter and son started at Tufts
in 1994 and 1996, I was astonished at the piles of expensive stuff that
came out of the parental caravan of cars, minivans, and SUVs. Kids
unloaded computers, televisions, small refrigerators, microwaves,
stereos, DVD players, video recorders, cell phones, hand-held electronic organizers, calculators, portable CD players, MP 3 players –
and Abercrombie big shirts and cargo pants, Doc Martins, North Face
jackets, and the like. Young adults are far from the only culprits. The
rest of us buy fast laptops, fine wine, expensive artwork, designer
clothes, spa vacations – and Jaguars. Money that goes for consumer
purchases keeps the wheels of capitalism humming, but it isn't available to buy the right kind of breathing room for people like Minga
and Roberto.

I don't come across too many people who are hoarders. I do know
of one. He and his wife operate a highly profitable rare antique business from their home. They live in a modest Cape Cod in a working-
class suburb, have one car between them, rarely eat out or travel,
don't buy much, and have no children. They don't give philan-
thropically – and aren't asked, since there are no visible signs that
they have money – other than a small contribution to the church col-
lection plate on Sundays. They accumulate money, the exact amount
known only to themselves, their estate attorney, and the IRS,
although surely now exceeding $10 million. Watching the number
grow, in and of itself, seems to give them great satisfaction. Hoarders
are the biggest puzzle to me; they work intensely hard to accumulate

a great power source, and then choose to leave it dormant. The main risk to the "money for me" crowd – the creators, consumers, and hoarders – is that the culture of success will translate in the end into a life of isolation and narrow purpose.

Sue and Lourdes and Muhammad Yunus believe in distributing money. Sue does it because she feels an obligation to give back. That's partly a family of origin value, and partly her own recognition of the assets she has been fortunate enough to amass. She doesn't find giving back intelligently an easy thing to do, because her heavy travel and work schedule leave little time for her to direct her money wisely. One of the kinds of "giving back" she enjoys most is mentoring younger women navigating a fast career track. She takes time to do that, and is good at it. They are, for the most part, well-educated and promising emerging talents – younger versions of her.

Lourdes gives of her money and her time out of a profound religious commitment to social justice. Her giving is directed toward the poor; she is not a financial supporter of such middle- and upper-class pursuits as the art gallery, the museum, and the symphony. She enjoys the arts, but figures they have a large enough pool of donors from which to draw. Her work on behalf of the church has not been easy. With her progressive theology, she is often at odds with a prevailing conservative clerical tide. She will not back away or be forced aside. It is her church, and she insists it stand with her to serve those who are struggling and in need.

Yunus distributes money to the poor through a for-profit financial institution as a business deal. He's come up with several operational practices that make lending to the poor successful enough so Grameen can thrive. Ninety- four per cent of the loans go to women. Early on, the Grameen bankers found that loans made to women radiate out from an individual family to benefit the whole community, creating what financial people call "leverage." Loans are made to people in small groups of five or so. One loan at a time is made to a group member; when that loan is repaid, someone else can borrow. Grameen's repayment rate has historically hovered around 95%. Grameen has given rise to various spin-offs, such as a partnership with GrameenPhone. GrameenPhone sells cellular telephones at modest prices to Grameen depositors in far-flung villages, providing them with a business opportunity and a way to connect isolated rural people with the rest of the world. This venture has caught the attention of our wired world; Grameen and GrameenPhone were profiled in the November 2000 *Industry Standard Grok.*

Grameen is far from perfect. Although the business model is built around depositors and borrowers who are primarily women, the bank has found hiring and retaining women employees difficult. Almost all those in higher-paying positions are men, although in 1997 Grameen appointed its first woman to the position of zonal manager. In his 1999 book *Banker to the Poor,* Yunus makes the case that this is not his preference, but a reflection of Bangladeshi culture that makes it hard for working women to be accepted by rural villagers among whom bank employees must travel seeking deposits and making loans.

Also, a loan from Grameen does not guarantee anyone a sustainable leg up on poverty. There is no safety net. Some of the loans work out and change the borrower's life over the long term; others fail. Grameen is a business, not a social service agency. The tentacles that keep people in poverty are winding and reluctant to let go their hold – even to a powerful development concept like micro-lending.

Finally, Grameen is based on a developing-country economic model that does not travel easily to more advanced economic models, such as ours. Owning a cell phone can really change the life of a rural Bangladeshi villager; the same is not true for her American counterpart. What does travel is the core concept that seems so at odds with much of American venture philanthropy: poor people get to decide, just like the rest of us did along the way, what's "better." The skill of making money, which those of us in the culture of success have mastered very well, is just that. Making money does not, in my view, create the right to use our money to embed a particular value set and definition of "success" into the lives of others.

The main risk for venture philanthropists – a segment of what we've identified as "distributors" – is that a lot of money can be given away without the donor experiencing what it means to really give, as in "ceding control." Part of the happiness that accrues to someone who gives away money is making it possible for other lives to flourish

freely. Retaining a high degree of control over someone else's outcomes can be distorting to both the recipient's opportunity to grow
and to the donor's experience of giving.

How Might "Money for We" Work Better?

My interest in making "money for we" work better comes from a deep
personal commitment. I also see an opportunity in the fact that I consult on business issues with a lot of clients who are awash in money,
yet seem to have a less clear sense of what to do with it than their parents or grandparents did. Part of the personal commitment comes
from my family of origin. While my sisters and I were young and my
mother was still a homemaker, she regularly volunteered at the hospital and at local nonprofit agencies. My father teased her for "running the only free taxi in town," as she would regularly jump in the
car to take elderly neighbors to do their grocery shopping. My father
was also committed to helping others in a quiet, behind-the-scenes
way. When he died, I was astonished at the number of people I did-
n't know who came to the wake, took my mother's hand, and poured
out their story of how "Mr. York helped me, and no one ever knew."

Part of the personal commitment also comes from my early religious formation in the Catholic Church of the 1950s. In after-school
catechism classes, we budding defenders of the faith were taught to
fill small cardboard mission boxes with money for the poor. When I
was in second or third grade the focus was an orphanage in China,
where for $5 worth of coins we could name a Chinese baby. I saved
prodigiously, filled several boxes, and named all the presumed recip-
ients "Barbara" after my sister who had died in infancy. I fervently
hope the "name a baby" part was pure marketing spin, as I'd be cha-
grined as an adult to think I had caused a Chinese woman to begin
life with such an American name. Notwithstanding that, the seed was
deeply planted in my young soul that whatever nickels and dimes
came my way were about something other than myself.

Perhaps most profoundly, the personal commitment comes from

my Peace Corps service. That morning over thirty years ago, when I pressed my face to the dirty window of the speeding Volkswagon bus and waved wildly back to Minga, I knew that leaving Rio Hato could never mean laying aside the shared commitments of our friendship.

Those commitments – creating economic lifelines, or standing for social justice, or what people of faith call "healing a broken world" – are tricky to implement. Effectively making money about "we," in my experience, takes three things. If any one is missing, the process falls apart. That process is built around three inseparably linked components:

People who want their lives to be different, and who will fight for that to happen.

Service providers who will work programmatically to provide skill training and emotional support to clients, and work systemically to help remove barriers to upward mobility.

Money.

People who are poor, and people who are economically stable but shunted to the sidelines for other reasons – such as mental illness – exist in abundance. Service providers who feel called to spend their lives helping others also exist in abundance. They themselves usually don't make very much money. Sometimes they're distinctly more talented at the softer skills of human interaction than at the business principles needed to alleviate Jane's and my concerns about how well nonprofits utilize resources.

The American culture of success, whether in a bull or bear market, is awash in money. People who are part of the culture of success are very good at knowing and applying business principles. We sometimes serve on nonprofit boards, often showing up at meetings sporadically as our travel and work schedules allow, but we often have neither time nor patience to be hands-on at helping remove systemic barriers through education, lobbying, or advocacy. Nor do we usually have much contact with people in the trenches who are actually fighting to change their lives.

It's terribly simplistic but true enough to say that "need" lives in one domain, the "willingness to serve" in another, and a good share of the required "money" in a third. To make money effectively about "we," bridges need to be built to connect the three domains. Perhaps the most sensible and meaningful contribution those of us who enjoy professional success and money can make is to commit to an ongoing role as "bridge builder."

A Model

Models give you ideas about what has worked in one place and what can be done elsewhere. What you're looking for, if you're intrigued by the role of bridge builder, is what can be done in your situation using the tools and channels close to your hand. The specifics of what someone else has done can help you understand the nitty-gritty of how a model unfolded, but are less important than your getting the core of an idea and using it to stimulate your own imagination about what can possibly be done.

Several years ago, I approached the board of the Women's Foundation of Genesee Valley, a nonprofit endowment that provides grant funding for programs that benefit women and girls. The foundation has a particular focus on supporting economic development for women who have not yet found their way to financial self-sufficiency. That mission has remained a particular passion for me ever since Panama. I see it as taking the basic idea of economic sustainability that so ignited the hopes of the Rio Hato villagers and planting that idea in new terrain. I served on the foundation's board at its inception, and have continued to be a "friend" of the foundation on an informal basis ever since. I approached the board in that role, on a pro bono basis, not as a paid consultant.

The concept I took to the foundation was called Rainmakers©, and I proposed that the foundation adopt Rainmakers© as a tool to build bridges. Those bridges would connect the foundation's goal of building a large pool of capital to support good projects, the need of service agencies to have stable sources of funding to help their clients, and professionally successful people – in this case mostly working women – with extra money.

Rainmakers© was built conceptually around five major points.

To appeal to people in the culture of success, the traditional story of philan-

thropic giving has to be wrapped in a new "big idea" – hence a name and a story like Rainmakers©." Rainmakers in the business world are those who use their larger-than-life prestige and professional track record to bring in work, which then gets sprinkled around and actually done by the merely competent players within law, accounting, and investment banking firms, ad agencies, and the like. Rainmakers© took that well-known concept and shifted it to mean "use your prestige and professional track record not to make money for yourself and for your organization, but to sprinkle a pool of resources around to benefit poor women." Rainmakers© were asked to give a one-time gift of $25,000, and to recruit another Rainmaker© who would give in that amount as well. Prior to that time, although the foundation had received some large gifts, most donations were in the range of $1,000 and under. In the first year of the Rainmakers© campaign, the Foundation closed eleven gifts of $25,000. In the second year the number grew to seventeen, and so on.

What made this big idea work with this particular population of donors? The project used a word with which they were familiar and which carries substantial prestige in the business world, then tweaked the meaning. That caught their attention. In a world where much of our day moves at warp speed and there is a constant information overload, getting people's attention is no small feat.

What you may notice is that the appeal of Rainmakers©, first, is about the donor, not the recipient. The message is, "You're successful, you're a player, now use that power to bring poor women into the economic system along with you." I can't tell you how many funding appeals I get in the mail which feature sick, hungry, hollow-eyed people and ask me to help with "any amount . . . $5 . . . $25 . . . $100 . . . or more." That's putting the need of the recipient first, and assuming it will prompt a check. Rainmakers© puts the self-interest of the donor first. That's consistent with my belief, and Art's, that people have to have their own needs met before they can consider the needs of others. Putting the donor first also represents my strongly pragmatic side coming to the fore. Visionaries, idealists, and prophets tend to want people to do the right thing for the right reason – and they'll wait if both action and intent aren't consistent. I'm content to ask someone to do the right thing – share part of his or her wealth – and trust that feeling and acting on empathy, if not originally present, may grow.

*People who live and work in the culture of success move at warp speed. If
you want them to do something for you, you have to move at warp speed too.*
A colleague of mine who is an expert professional fundraiser calls the
process leading up to a big gift "romancing the donor." First there's
an introduction – probably over lunch – then an invitation to come
and see the workings of the agency, then a request for a first gift, then
an attempt to get the donor more involved, and then, finally, "the big
ask." All of that can take months, or even longer. In my experience,
such a process is too long and too slow to appeal to hard-pressed corporate executives, professionals, or business owners. Once you have
their attention, you need to move fast. We ask potential Rainmakers©
for their commitment on a first – and often only – meeting. I closed
one Rainmaker© when she and I were sitting on a grassy hill at an outdoor concert. She mentioned wanting to do something philanthropic for a local women's organization, but had real reservations
about their operating efficiency and effectiveness. I responded with
"In that case, I have an idea that might intrigue you," and closed the
deal right then and there, just on the power of the story – no glitzy
marketing materials or invitations to "come and visit the foundation."

*People in the culture of success think big, and want to make a big foot-
print.* Rainmakers© responded to that value by instituting a "big ask,"
an initial commitment of $25,000. People who are part of this culture
also tend to have short attention spans; if you get their attention, you
may well only have it until the next big idea comes along. This isn't a
case of gradually building a relationship, then looking for the larger
financial gifts to come over time. This is a case of getting in, getting
what you need, and moving on.

*People in the culture of success want to run at the head of the pack, and
care very much whether or not "the pack" is the right pack.* Clearly, we knew
it would matter to prospective Rainmakers© who their giving coun-
terparts would be. Recognizing that, we placed the responsibility for
finding another Rainmaker© on each donor. Simply put, if they
wanted the right crowd, they'd have to go out and help us build it.
The strategy has worked well, with one interesting twist. One donor
was so unsettled by the thought of asking someone for money in a
philanthropic context – although in her business life she negotiates

deals all the time – that she chose to donate $50,000 to cover her own commitment and that of a phantom "other."

Successful people care about success, and want to be involved with projects that are financially successful. If your organization is on its last legs and you're looking for money to keep you from having to shut the doors, that's not a condition that will appeal much to this population. Even if your coffers are thin, you have to find a way to make your story look and sound big and successful enough to change the world, or at least a corner of it.

What's in All of This for You?

There were other factors that made Rainmakers© successful, such as a very talented executive director and a board willing to take a risk on a new idea. The foundation also supports programs that involve women in critical decisions about their lives, which is consistent with my philosophy that people get to decide what "better" means. Identifying every last factor that made Rainmakers© work isn't important. What matters is your getting the idea of what being a bridge builder means, and going out and trying something yourself. Here are the steps you need to think about most:

Figure out what you can do and are willing to do to help others at this stage in your professional life. In the jargon of the culture of success, that's called "identifying your value-add."

> What are three things you can do really well? Mine are: a brain hardwired to come up with big ideas, contact with men and women who have money, and the ability to tell a compelling story.
>
> What are three things you don't want to do right now, especially when you're giving your time pro bono? Mine are: sit through long nonprofit board or committee meetings, be responsible for the operational details of a project, or motivate a board to take a risk – I want to work with people who are already motivated, and looking for the right move.

If you're clear about your own "upside" and your own "downside," you'll be able to structure a role that fits your talents, time availability, and interests.

Know why you want to make your professional success and your money about "we," and integrate that with your chosen bridge-building project. If your commitment to others is religious in nature, take time to explore what your faith tradition teaches about giving. If your commitment is based on wanting to get to know people who are different from you, make sure your project brings you into direct contact with the clients being served. If you want an experience that goes beyond what you do every day, make sure your role in the project doesn't replicate your work role. If you want to leverage what you already know so you don't have to spend the time to master new skills, make sure your role does replicate your success at work. If you take time to integrate your beliefs, your own psychological needs, and the project, your experience will be far more satisfying.

Go against your own impatience and risk making a real commitment to a project. Just like at work, your big idea will sooner or later run into roadblocks and problems. If you start a ball rolling, don't abandon it at the first sign of trouble. Don't give yourself an easy out because this is, after all, "something extra" you're doing, and you need to give priority to your paid work. If you make a commitment to have your money be about "we," that means "long enough to make some real difference."

Practice letting go. You got where you are now, in part, because you're really good at holding on: to your focus, to multiple tasks, to managing relationships, and to driving toward completion. Making money about "we" means letting go of some part of your resources in the interests of supporting other people who are fighting to identify and follow their own path. Don't sit on their shoulders while they do it, trying to steer them in what you are sure is the right direction. There's joy enough in watching someone else decide whether to bunt, go for consistent singles, or look toward the bleachers and swing.

You've made the money; if you want it to be about "me," so be it. The risks you take are that you'll wind up alone, or with people who only care about you because you have money and they might get some, and that your life may seem to have little enduring meaning. If you want your money to be about "we," keep in mind the triangle of need/service providers/resources. Figure out where your particular talents can best be used in building bridges. Understand that "money for we" is about practicing a skill that's very hard for successful people: letting go.

CHAPTER SEVEN

Money Decisions: "Right, Wrong, and Relative"

CREATING A MATURE MONEY story has yet another hard element: developing a framework for assessing the "right, wrong, or relative" of a money decision. In the last chapter I referred to the closing of the Rio Hato cattle operation as a decision that was "probably right, but one that didn't feel very good." As you've gotten more deeply into exploring money's power, role dilemmas, and possible purposes, you're likely to have come across an uncomfortable truth. Money decisions, carefully arrived at and implemented, do not always feel right. They can also have aspects that feel unsettlingly relative, distasteful, or even wrong. Examples are easy to find.

When you're hard on the track of big money and professional success, your relationships with people, on both a personal and a professional level, can take on a "utilitarian" or "transactional" quality. If you have any time and energy beyond immediate family obligations and job requirements, you may well come to the decision that you need to spend those precious extra moments with "the right people." That means people who can help advance your interests in some way, and you theirs. While such a utilitarian exchange can bring big rewards, there's also something sacrificed. You lose a considerable amount of spontaneity and diversity when you become so intentional about the people with whom you interact.

When you have big money and professional success, you get to throw your weight around. You sometimes have to draw lines in the sand that affect other people in an unwelcome way. Your actions may be correct in a logical sense, and right in a moral sense, yet they impinge on the choices of others – sometimes others who are quite close to you.

When you deal with big money, you come across bad actors. Big money draws amoral people as surely as an open honey pot draws bees. You can do your best to avoid or work around such people, but sooner or later count on winding up in a project or a deal with one. Then you have to figure out how to proceed as best you can, or extricate yourself, without losing your integrity or sacrificing the interests of your clients, investors, students, or patients.

When you deal with big money, you come across good people doing a bad job coping with mistakes. People sometimes begin a venture with the best of intentions and with utmost integrity. When matters go awry, they try to get out of a bad spot by protecting themselves first. No one, after all, wants to appear publicly inept. As in the case of bad actors, you have to figure out how to go forward in compromised situations without sacrificing your own values or the values of the people you represent.

As you integrate money's hardest questions into your everyday life, you'll meet these "right, wrong, and relative" moments more frequently than you may have expected. Don't think they're the exception; they're quite common, especially if you're on a fast track professionally and money is important to you. Let's see if we can develop some rules of the road that will help you make the best decision possible when these kinds of hard moments arise.

"Dear Friend and Colleague – What Have You Done for Me Lately?"

When the demands on your time become intense, your relationships can take on a utilitarian cast. With so little time to spare, you want relationships beyond your immediate circle of family and close friends to "do something" for you. For those of us who value a spirit of generosity toward others, or for those of us who have been helped along the way and acknowledge a responsibility to "give back," or for people who simply like diversity in their lives, reaching points where we require relationships to meet a "utility" standard is a hard moment.

For most of my career, I've made myself available for what people call "networking interviews." Usually such requests come on referral from someone who knows me, who is asking that I give brief pro bono professional advice to one of their colleagues, friends, or family members. In responding, I'm actually giving back in two ways: once to a person likely to be unknown to me, and again to the friend or colleague who has made the request.

During a period when I'm writing intensely, I create a major exception to that rule. When I'm working on a book, I prefer to immerse myself in the project with the fewest possible distractions. That means dramatically restricting my availability to others for months at a time, especially to people unknown to me. My director of operations has a standard reply for anyone making a request that is unrelated to the book: she tells the inquirer that I'm on sabbatical and gives the date when I will return full-time to the office. The requests don't even come to my attention. While working on this book, I did get a direct email inquiry from someone seeking my advice on a matter of great importance to her. She listed the names of several people I know who had assured her that I was the best person to help her at this critical moment. She told me her need was time-limited; she was facing several decisions in the near future that, once made, would be hard to unwind. I responded with the standard "on sabbatical," wished her well in her rapid decision process, and said I regretted being unable to meet with her until several months hence. She emailed back two or three more times, asking if she could take me to lunch or dinner, have the referring colleagues call, or if there might be some other way I could be persuaded to find time for her. Getting no response, she finally sent me a letter in which she told me, among other things, that she simply couldn't believe I was unable to find even a moment for her in my life. The tone of the letter sounded quite testy.

Unwittingly perhaps, she had come close to the hard truth. Relative to the time and focus I need to write well, meeting with her was not important to me – as it might have been at another time. I didn't know her as a person, and she was not in a position to help me advance the book project. I chose not to extend generosity to a stranger, and there was no visible opportunity for a utilitarian exchange. We did not meet.

Others who lead time-compacted lives speak of different facets of the same choice. One corporate president spoke of the need to "be on the right boards, be seen as part of the right organizations – side by side with other people in the city who count." An ambitious CEO spoke of the need to be associated with "people of a similar power base." The utilitarian exchange, in these cases, is of status and power – surely important commodities for people on a fast upward track.

What I'm calling a "utilitarian exchange" in relationships is different from the normal boundary-setting to which all of us are entitled. No one, in my view, is obligated to sacrifice personal or professional energy willy-nilly to anyone who wants a piece of us. I'm talking about the case beyond normal boundary-setting, where people who live by the values of the culture of success subtly keep our antennae alert to the "value-add" in a prospective relationship. In terms of availability, this is not exactly what most of us grew up with as a "golden rule" of treating others in the way one would like to be treated. Nor is it anything close to the biblical concept of "agape," which roughly describes love that exists solely for itself, without the expectation of return. Nor is it particularly consistent with the kind of working-class communities novelist Zora Neale Hurston wrote about, where people lived, worked, ate, drank, played, suffered, and simply survived together. This utilitarian exchange is, however, what many successful people come to see as a necessary component of a fast-track life.

Jon is 23, single, and a new financial consultant for a major brokerage firm. He describes his family origins as "upper class." His father is a successful entrepreneur who values education, the moral values of goodness and decency, and giving to others. The family has a charitable foundation through which it annually gives away what Jon calls "substantial money." Jon also gives charitably in his own right – not at the same level, clearly, but at a level that stretches his current earnings.

Jon values success, and plans to be a success. He greatly respects his father's career path and is able to hear and learn from his father's wisdom. Listening to Jon recount his father's advice, I'd say his father knows about "utilitarian exchange" – not, as Jon says, in a "snobbish sense," but as a reality of doing business.

On graduating from college, Jon gave some thought to living with his former roommate in an apartment near the campus. Jon's father took him aside and suggested a different direction. As Jon remembers, his father's counsel went along these lines:

> College was great, college was fun, but it's time to move on now. You're in the business world, and you need to be in the professional world on every level. You want to be associating with professional people your own age, dressing nicely, moving into the type of circles where you're going to be doing business. If you're going to eat at fast food chains and college bars and sub shops, you're not going to find your clients at those sorts of places. You need to act and dress the part of someone who can show his clients he isn't intimidated by money.

Jon chose a different set of housemates – ambitious guys with good jobs in a different neighborhood. The choice was a better fit with his personal and professional direction. I asked him how the decision felt.

> My Dad wasn't making a judgment on people who wear flip flops and look for bars with $1 draft beers. My friends that I live with now do that. My Dad was saying that it's important to associate in the types of circles where I'm going to find the right kinds of people. I actually find decisions about relationships harder on the business side. It's tough to find good clients. Would I love 100 clients all worth $10M? Yes, but would I want to take them all? Probably not. Money changes people. Money hardens people, lets them think they're better than other individuals and that doesn't feel good. I've only been in the business a short while, but I have one or two clients who certainly aren't people I'd befriend if I weren't doing business with them. Are they good for a business relationship? Absolutely. So there's a kind of tugging and pulling on each side.

Jon's father helped illuminate a hard truth. If you want to advance in the world, you have to associate with people who have achieved the level of success to which you aspire. That way, the right kinds of exchanges are possible.

"Looking to what a relationship can do for you" occurs on both the personal side and on the business side, and in settings far more diverse than Jon's demanding task of building a successful brokerage clientele. Professionals who work to a billable-hours model juggle what the client authentically needs and can pay for with the mandate to have their time 75% or 80% billable. An April 2001 *New York Times* article reported on the annual management conference of the American Association of Advertising Agencies [the Four A's]. Maurice Levy, chairman and chief executive officer of the Paris-based Publicis Groupe, challenged his fellow advertising executives to consider whether the industry had contributed to the rapid decline of the dot.com world – along with investment bankers – by providing services more distinguished by their high fees and too-elaborate campaigns than by sound business counsel.

The tension extends beyond the financial and "billable hours" worlds. People in the media business juggle purchasing decisions about subtle and complex work with their knowledge of what the mass market will subscribe to, watch, listen to, or buy. Educational administrators juggle criteria for admission with the need to have tuition-paying students on the rolls. At one financially struggling graduate institution where I taught as an adjunct, one of my adult students had been accepted for master's level work on a provisional basis, without having completed his bachelor's degree. The school needed the tuition and the warm body to help meet minimum class size requirements. The man completed the course work for his M.A. degree and then lost his job. The M.A. couldn't be conferred until he completed his B.A., for which he had no money. He left the institution in search of a new job with no degree in hand at all, with only his high school diploma plus "considerable college level and graduate study" to claim on a job application. I call that "Dear friend or colleague or client or student or patient, how can you help me meet my productivity targets today?"

I've proposed creating guidelines to help you make decisions when such difficult moments arise. Those guidelines, in the case of relationships marked by utilitarian exchange, are hard to nail down. I know, as many of us know, that some of our most profound personal moments have come with people very different from us, with whom there is no "performance expectation" or obligation to pay back, and who tolerate more than admire our drive for success. I know that the best professional relationships happen among people who can cut each other some slack, who know that not every transaction will wind up even approximately balanced. I also know, whether the original stimulus for forming a relationship was utilitarian or not, that once I'm involved with someone he or she becomes a real person to me, not someone easy to brush aside when the business value of the exchange diminishes.

Balancing those insights with the need to be judicious about time and "relationship value", my rules of the road are these:

Make a list of the people you know, beyond immediate or extended family, with whom you'd commit to keeping a relationship, regardless of how that person's ability to do things for you might change. I'm intentionally not making a distinction here between "work friends" and "personal friends," because for people who mostly work "friends" of any kind are mostly connected in some way to work. If hardly anyone makes your list, you may have taken "utilitarian exchange" farther than is safe. You may have blurred or erased a boundary that needs to be redrawn. Professional relationships are, in large measure, appropriately utilitarian or transactional; people come together for a specific purpose, and move on when that purpose has been completed. Launching an IPO, for example, brings together investment bankers, accountants, attorneys, senior management from the company seeking to become public, and members of regulatory agencies. People brought together around the IPO, for a specific and intense period, may work together, eat together, have drinks, or jog together at the end of the day, and even share confidences. In short, they do many of the same things people who have an ongoing relationship may do. Yet, when the deal is done, it's done. Most of the people move on. Those who keep the relationship going often do it for a specific, utilitarian purpose; there may be other deals on which collaboration and mutual profit can happen.

If you agree that part of "feeling safe" in your professional and personal life has to do with people you can count on, you need to go beyond utilitarian exchange. Form real friendships or find an enduring colleague or two – someone you can rely on even if one or both of your situations change. That kind of person doesn't go away easily, because the work of building intimacy is never done. Just don't confuse real intimacy with "trading services." Real intimacy takes time and commitment from both of you. Real intimacy takes altruism – the willingness, from time to time, to put the other person's interests before your own. Real intimacy can only happen with people who acknowledge and share feelings – often a threat to the "suck it up" norms and fast pace of the culture of success.

Recognize your own human vulnerabilities. If you never needed anything beyond a business transaction to be happy in life, you wouldn't have to concern yourself with relationships that stick. Because we all have vulnerabilities – even those of us who are proud of our "steel spines" – we do need support, help, and tiding-over from time to time. At this moment you may be flying high, running at the head of the pack, celebrating your golden touch. That's great. It also won't last forever; a golden touch never does. If you're only interesting to people – and they to you – when you shine in a brilliant light, you're on very shaky long-term ground.

Be careful of "just until." The most common phrase people use when they want to maintain a pattern of behavior is to say "I'm doing this just until . . . just until I launch the company . . . sell the company . . . get tenure . . . build up my practice . . . get our operating budget in the black . . . nail the first really big win." Or whatever. "Just until" is dangerous for two reasons. The first is that patterns that become very deeply ingrained over a long period of time become increasingly harder to change. If you race around mostly solo for much of your life, learning to lean on others – as you may have to do if you or someone close to you becomes ill, injured, disabled, or simply old – isn't going to come easily. The second reason is that no one is guaranteed the "until." Those of us who have experienced the sudden death of someone we love know that all we have for sure is the moment we're in. Deferring real intimacy until you have more time is a lonely and high-risk game.

What if your problem is the reverse – that you're not utilitarian enough, unable to set boundaries, or guard your time and energy at all? Phil Porter and Cynthia Winton-Henry are performance artists, founders of Bay-area Interplay and Body Wisdom Inc., and ordained ministers. Ministers, and others in healing professions, often find it hard to say "no" to people who need them, even to the point of physical exhaustion and burnout. Of that, Winton-Henry says:

> Some of us tend to overintegrate what we feel called to do professionally, and carry our commitments around like a burden. What might work better is to relate to our commitments as something clearly outside of us. I think it enough to simply carry my own purpose. Releasing our burdens is about rearranging how we physically hold onto things. It is my belief that we are not required to hold onto too many things. Maybe there is just one basic but unique truth we are each meant to hold on to – our life purpose.

If you find yourself focusing almost exclusively on the needs of others, try giving yourself a break. Take time to describe, in actual words, your own purpose in life. Do you know clearly enough what that purpose is, and are you honoring your own life's purpose in the way you spend you time and creative energy? If not, what changes do you need to make – right now, not "just until . . ."?

"Big Money + Success = Big Weight to Throw Around"

The second really hard truth about money and success is that they allow you – sometimes encourage you – to throw your weight around. What you make happen might very well be a good thing, the correct thing, even the morally right thing. It just may not sit very well with others, sometimes those "others" are people quite close to you – family or friends or colleagues that you have to deal with every day.

Here's what throwing your weight around in a public setting sounds like:

> I frequently have used my power to put people in their place, or to keep them in their place, to remind them that they should not go where I am. There are people in this community who believe I might not be capable of a contract where I would win and they would not. Or, that we would sign a contract whose benefit we would share equally. More than once I have walked away from the table and not flinched until they came back – because I was in the ultimately more powerful position. They're arrogant to assume that because

> they've been here longer than I have, they could prevail. These are people used to getting their own way, and I was not as significant a player in their minds as I was in my own. So it became a surprise to them.

Author Peter Bloch writes about a concept he calls "servant leadership" – a way of leading in which the individual in the top position is at the service of an organization, a profession, a group of constituents. Is "knowing how to throw your weight around when necessary" consistent with the feeling, tone, and values of servant leadership? Probably not. Is such behavior an important leadership skill in the culture of success? Yes. Running at the head of the pack – in business, in politics, in religious organizations, in large nonprofits, in health care, and in higher education – is a big stakes game, rough in its jockeying for place and not well-suited to the temperaments of servant souls. "Throwing your weight around" can be thought of in a number of ways, such as "jockeying for position," "holding your ground," "gaining ground," or "having you interests prevail." It has to do with a forward, thrusting energy and with truth candidly conveyed, with or without the softening laid on by social graces. In all cases, the behavior is about the individual and the organization – the individual getting respect, recognition, and the kind of deference normally accorded those who are perceived as players, the organization getting the ground it needs to grow. Both are necessary in the culture of success, but throwing your weight around has consequences. You can make enemies. You can also badly intimidate those with whom you work most closely, like your senior management team. They may fear that the hard-nosed behavior they see playing itself out among you and your leadership peers can, at a different time, be turned on them.

The culture of success tends to accept leaders who throw their weight around under two conditions, which might be viewed as part of our ground rules. The leader must be successful in running his or her endeavor, and the taking of ground must be seen as happening within aggressive but fair limits. T. J. Rogers of Cypress Semiconductors comes to mind as an example of a leader who pushes the edge, but with a defensible position. As for leaders who brag about a "scorched earth" management style, when they fall, they fall hard – witness the rise and rapid plummet from public view of "Chainsaw Al" Dunlap, former CEO of Sunbeam.

Most of us are less comfortable throwing our financial weight around on private, personal matters, especially with regard to family members. An executive with a six-figure compensation package has supplemented her aging mother's income for years. A person with poor conflict resolution skills, the mother frequently fell into arguments with landlords and neighbors, often moving on the spur of the moment. As often as every six months, the executive and her siblings picked up moving costs, bought and sold appliances depending on what was in the latest apartment, tried to negotiate for cleaning and other support services in yet another location. The mother's housing choices became increasingly questionable in terms of neighborhood. Finally, the executive gave her mother a choice: move into an assisted living facility, for which the executive would pay, or the annual stipend would stop and her mother would be on her own. The executive sighed as she sat in front of me. "I don't know whether or not I did the right thing. I feel better knowing that my mother is in a safe place, that her heat and electricity are provided, that she is served three meals a day, and someone is around to check on her if she doesn't show up one morning. But I know my mother is mentally competent to make her own decisions, and this move was not her choice. I hit her over the head with a financial club to make her go into assisted living. She hates feeling stuck in one place. She tells me she feels as if she's in jail."

When we assume responsibility for our financial choices and at least in principle honor the right of others to choose, we come up against hard moments. Money decisions – even those carefully thought-out – do not always feel right. Money decisions can also feel wrong or relative. "Relative" means we simply don't know whether or not we did the right thing, because we can see right on more than one side. When we throw our financial clout around within our families, or with those who are closest to us, we can arouse ire, resentment, and guilt – or endless expectations. I once worked with an older couple whose three adult offspring, all well-educated, married, and working, still hit up their parents for "emergencies" such as broken water heaters, snow tires, and car repairs. Perhaps, on an unconscious level, the couple relished their continued role as active parents and their importance in their adult daughters' lives. On another level, they were becoming increasingly annoyed and frustrated at the constant, nagging demands. After our work together, the parents decided to stop responding to the repeated requests for budgetary bailouts. In order to accomplish that goal, given the expectations that had become set over a period of more than ten years, the parents and I worked out a six-month transition. Each adult daughter was given a fixed sum at the outset, with the suggestion that she budget the money for unanticipated, one-time expenses. At the end of the six- month period, there would be no more money forthcoming, and the young families would have to provide for contingencies on their own. The parents explained the new rules with care and compassion, but also with honesty about their own growing resentment. One daughter responded graciously, one was cool, and the third was, at least initially, quite put out.

"Throwing your weight around" on a personal level means using your financial power to move matters in what you perceive to be a right and necessary direction. Sometimes that behavior impinges on the choices of others. Sometimes it creates bad feelings. No matter; if you have the financial heft and are willing to use it, your judgment will most likely prevail. That's a big responsibility, one that you need to exercise with care and intention.

Here are some questions for double-checking your own behavior when you feel yourself ready to exert financial clout.

What's the outcome you're trying to achieve? How much of that outcome represents a legitimate business or personal goal, and how much is fueled by your wanting payback ?

It's natural and human to feel angry when someone treats you badly. Still, your action should be motivated in larger measure by the desire for a good outcome, not by the need for retaliation or revenge. Have a serious conversation between you and you – between your competing motivations – and decide where the larger truth lies.

Is the action you propose to take fair? Could you sit across from the person or people who will be affected and explain what's happening, and why?

If not – if you need someone to do the explaining for you – I suggest that your action is suspect, even in your own mind.

Can you live with the long-term consequences of your action?

When you throw your weight around, you're trying to make something happen that you perceive to be good – at least good for you, and perhaps for others. "Good" almost always comes with trailing complex emotions and with unintended consequences. Can you truly live with whatever shakes out after you've made your move, without becoming resentful or bitter?

Big Money and Bad Actors

Just like a honey pot attracts bees, big money attracts amoral people, what I call colloquially "bad actors." During the ten years that I served as president of our brokerage firm – especially between 1981 and 1986, when the tax code was extremely favorable for tax shelters – Jerry and I brokered a number of leveraged real estate deals. That's where I really came to know firsthand what "bad actor" means.

"Leveraged" means a real-estate developer puts down a little of his own money to make the deal happen; the rest comes from other sources, usually banks or private investors.

Brokerage firms bring together the developer, the deal (mostly low-income housing projects, in our case), and the investors in a way that's consistent with federal and state securities regulations. "Investors" can be anyone qualified by level of financial assets to participate. "Extremely favorable" means there was a lot of money to be made in good deals – by the real estate developers, by firms like ours, and by investors – simply by being smart about the tax code. But along with mostly honorable players looking to make the most of what Congress had wrought came the sharks. We avoided most of them, but not all.

This experience- the one I know best – gives me a specific way of talking about compromised people and the situations they create. I write from my own observations, not from actual interviews or conversations. Bad actors don't line up to appear in books, mostly because they don't often acknowledge doing anything wrong. I suspect the principles I've learned hold true in most professional settings, not just the securities business. Take a moment here, before you read further, to consider what a "bad actor" might look like in your profession. That will give you your own context, your own way of thinking about bad actors in the setting you know best.

How does a bad actor (hopefully someone you've learned to give a wide berth) differ from someone in your field who is merely aggressive, competitive, and out to win? What we're talking about is a convergence of the following set of circumstances:

Something that sounds too good to be true

People who want to believe in the "too good to be true" opportunity

An amoral individual who provides the container for everyone's hopes.

Money is the common denominator, the currency of hope, the element that draws all sides to the party.

We've talked about "containers" in an earlier chapter. Money creates containers. Both good people and amoral people can create containers – and sometimes, at the outset, it's difficult to tell them apart even with careful screening. Bad actors can often be charming and persuasive. They can skate on the surface of accountability for a long time. Sometimes, just when they're revealed at their worst, there will be certain stakeholders at some distance from the day-to-day action – boards of directors, trustees, regulators, or funders – who continue to see them as wonderful.

In your professional career, have you run across anyone like that? In your professional career, have you ever played the role of the bad actor? Do you know why you chose to go there? Are you still there? If not, what motivated you to change?

The "container," in our case as a brokerage firm, was a real estate deal brought to us by the developer. A "container" might also be a grant application, a business alliance, a start-up company, a philanthropic opportunity, a chance to expand the scope and mission and funding of an agency, a funded research project, a media deal – anything that involves large sums of money.

How then, in most professional settings, does an aggressive but ethical player differ from a bad actor?

Aggressive players pay careful attention to written contracts, letters of agreement, and other legal documents that set out the terms of the project. They do so because they intend two things. They intend to carve out the maximum benefit they can for themselves. And, they ultimately intend to honor what they've agreed to in terms of benefit to other participants. Bad actors pay very little attention to the written agreements. They just want the deal done so they can get started with whatever the project entails, and they don't intend to honor what they've agreed to anyway.

Aggressive players, at the outset of the project, carve out meaningful fees for themselves. By getting as much money as they can up front, the aggressive player has much less risk relative to the long-term success of the project. On the positive side, where all the money will go is clearly spelled out from the start. Bad actors settle for what they can up front. They go into the agreement knowing they're going to exploit every loophole they can find – and they're practiced at finding loopholes – to try and strip as much benefit as they can out of the project once it's underway. That behavior often endangers the long-term success of the venture, destroying or sharply reducing the value for other participants.

Aggressive players deliver on the deal they've agreed to. When there's a dispute about the interpretation of any specific clause or agreement, they're conceptually fair. Presented with a logical case, they can be reasonable. In the end, they'll compromise rather than drag the project down in a way that benefits no one. Bad actors disregard key terms of the deal until caught. A major characteristic of bad actors is uncontrolled greed. They rationalize everything in their own favor, and are shocked and wounded when someone questions their behavior. They rush to defend themselves with numerous and often spurious legal challenges, all of which have to be answered. Having to call in legal firepower to uphold the terms of an agreement with a bad actor is always a costly, time-consuming, and frustrating process.

Again, I'd ask you to pause. Think about what you've identified as distinguishing an aggressive player from a bad actor in your work life. How do amoral people drawn to your profession behave? What makes it hard to nail them, even when you and others see clearly what's going on?

Rules of the road for dealing with bad actors are clear:

Avoid them at all costs when you can. If something sounds too good to be true, it probably is. You've heard that before, and it's still true. Check carefully on the reputation and operating history of people with whom you choose to work. In the securities business, that's called "due diligence"; in your professional life, it's probably called something else. Be wary; listen as much for what references don't say as what they do say. If someone or some aspect of the project raises the hairs on the back of your neck, don't let the prospect of money lead you to disregard your instincts and experience. Chances are you'll pay dearly in the end.

If you've been snookered, get out if you can. Sometimes getting out is very difficult. You may be representing the interests of others who can't walk away. You may have trouble getting the facts you need to make a good decision or to verify what you suspect. The bad actor may have built certain protections into project that make it hard to remove him or his organization. You may really, really want what you think the bad actor still has to offer – even if the promised payback has remained totally elusive so far.

If you have to stay in the project, watch the bad actor like a hawk. Verify everything he tells you independently and with great fanfare – especially the financials – so he understands he's being monitored. This will probably eat up any financial gain you expected to make. Consider it a cost of doing business – the price of a learning experience, like getting an M.B.A..

Buy the bad actor out. If he's a relatively small-time bad actor, squeezing an extra $15,000 or $20,000 or $50,000 out of a multimillion dollar project, it may be more cost-effective in the long run to buy out his interest. Doing so may be expensive, and may cause you to grind your teeth at the unfairness. It may also be the most financially effective way to protect your longer-term interests and those of the other participants.

There's a certain rough justice that seems to befall bad actors. Perhaps surprisingly, amoral people are often highly susceptible to the manipulation of bigger, more sophisticated sharks. They ultimately become the victim of the very thing they have supplied to others – a promise too good to be true. By that time, they've usually hurt a lot of people and left a lot of turbulence in their wake.

Good People Acting Badly

People sometimes begin a project with the best of intentions to do something good and expect to act with the utmost integrity. When matters go awry, they try to get out of a bad spot by adopting a "CYA" (cover your ass) mentality. Their motivation for doing what they do is very different from that of a bad actor – good people just don't want to be seen as publicly inept – but the end result is similar. You wind up in a compromised situation.

The common denominator, again, is money. Money – and the promise of money in terms of bringing recognition, advancement, and meaningful change – always draws people into its orbit. I write again from my own experience, while inviting you to reflect with me on yours. That gives what we come up with a more universal meaning than the story of a single life, a particular profession, or a discrete event.

Early in my consulting career, after I had left the active practice of financial planning, I was asked by an attorney to work with a group of very low-income residents who were about to become owners of their housing project. Although I work mostly with highly successful entrepreneurs and executives, I always have one very different kind of project in my consulting portfolio. That's to keep me aware that the whole world doesn't run on fast forward time. I accepted the job. The attorney, who had his own small practice, focused on what I would call "public interest law"; he worked mostly with poor people and with nonprofit agencies serving the poor on issues like housing rights, evictions, unfair lending practices, repossession of property, and the like. In this case, he was involved with an innovative and promising vision. A governmental funding body, a nonprofit housing agency, and a private developer skilled in rehabilitating old properties had come together with the attorney to transform an abandoned inner-city school building into thirty or so bright, airy, spacious condominiums. Each resident would own his or her particular unit, and the condominium association, to which each owner belonged by right, would own the building and the land on which it rested. Once trained, an elected resident council would act as the governing body, setting up committees to screen prospective new owners, collect rents, hire and

supervise a management company to handle the day-to-day operations, resolve tenant disputes, work with the local police on security
issues in their rough neighborhood, and act as ongoing intermediary
between the funding body and the resident group as a whole. Once
title to the property was transferred from the nonprofit agency to the
residents, the agency would withdraw and move on to another project.

When I began working with the resident council, the project was
already a year old and every condominium unit was occupied. The
units were spacious and bright – many of the residents said it was the
nicest home they'd ever known. They desperately wanted the project
to work, and members of the resident council were willing to show
up at long training meetings to make that happen, often with small
children in tow. Title had not yet been transferred. A condition of
transferring ownership to the residents was that the property had to
be breaking even in its operation; so far, that target had been elusive.

Who are "very low-income" urban people? Some of them have debilitating illnesses or injuries, and are living on Social Security disability
income. One woman, a leader in the condominium group, had been
battling a severe case of lupus for over twenty years. One man had been
hit on the head by a falling chunk of concrete while walking under an
old railroad overpass; he was left with a $10,000 settlement and an inabil-
ity to concentrate for very long. One couple came to meetings in their
motorized wheelchairs, operated by hand controls. Although the building was handicapped-accessible, the automatic door to the laundry
room was activated by pushing a large button on the wall that they had
great difficulty reaching. Although their neighbors were gracious about
helping, if the couple was in the laundry room and someone forgot to
come at the arranged time to open the door, they were stranded. Some
very low-income people take the bus to work every day, but don't earn
enough to support their families. Some have come through failing
school systems, and have the reading and math capabilities of a fourth
or fifth grader; they participate in the job market as best they can. Being
poor is no measure of one's longing for a better life, especially for the
children; these residents had that in abundance.

My first task was to get up to speed on the terms of the deal. I had
left behind the practice of financial planning, but not the skills

involved in reading and assessing an offering memorandum that governed the relationships between each individual resident, the resident group as a whole, and the funder. As is typically the case, the inch-and-a-half thick document was filled with legalese and long operating expense projections. Each resident, supposedly having read and accepted the terms, had signed one.

I remember reading with a growing sense of déjà vu, and thinking of Rio Hato. This project wasn't going to work, and not because the residents weren't trained enough or weren't trying. The project wasn't going to work because the money wasn't there to operate it at break even. Offering memoranda are written before the project is built and state the operating expenses as they can best be anticipated. In this case, the project was already a year old, and had a twelve-month track record of operating costs. The high ceilings and huge, sealed, classroom-style windows gave the units their bright and airy feeling. They also made the space horrendously expensive to heat and air-condition – hundreds of dollars more a month than had been projected. Very low-income people have no capacity to come up with an extra few hundred a month; the money simply isn't there. An amount of $100,000 had been set aside in the overall operating budget for capital improvements – a pittance for an old building of this size whose owners would have no capacity to contribute to replenishing that fund. Some $60,000 had already been spent postconstruction on additional security fencing, gates, and better outdoor lighting to protect residents' comings and goings and to shield their children playing on the grounds. The hallway carpets – a moderate industrial grade – were already showing signs of hard wear, and the replacement cost would eat up more than the remaining $40,000. The examples went on and on.

The unfolding of this story, as you can imagine, was long and convoluted, but can be made short. There were no bad actors here, only good people who, having steered into an iceberg, were trying desperately not to sink. Once convinced of the underlying financial issue, the agency decided to renegotiate quietly with the funder to change the terms of the project so that prospective residents could include "moderate-income" people. Over time, as each low-income resident found his or her unit too costly to maintain, a family with a bit more income would be the replacement. Why did the agency take that course of action? The business of winning funding from a governmental body is highly competitive. The agency felt that, by dealing quietly with officials identified as sympathetic, they would avoid the shame of having to say openly, "Look, we really miscalculated here, but we won't do it on our next application. You can trust us."

The lawyer specifically forbade me to tell the residents the project didn't look like it was going to work financially. He told me that I had been hired to train the resident council to assume legal title to the property, and that making judgments on longer-term financial viability was well outside the scope of my contract with him and the agency. Strictly speaking, that was probably true. Why did he take that course of action? He seemed like a good and socially committed person; I think he didn't want to appear publicly inept. I suspect his legal expertise was in contract law, not in securities law, and that he lacked enough experience with this type of venture to tell whether the projected financials had any reality to them at all. In short, he'd been snookered by numbers too good to be true.

What did I do? I worked with the resident council for the designated year, trying as hard as possible to make the numbers simple so they would see for themselves why things weren't going to work. They didn't really see, or didn't want to see. They kept focusing on things like preventing graffiti on the outside walls – important, but in this case akin to shifting deck chairs on the *Titanic*. Like most of us, perhaps the ones who did understand were hoping life would cut them a break for once and it would all work out anyway, just because they wanted it so much. We also focused on the rest of the issues: how you hire a management company, what you expect of them, how you resolve resident disputes when the offending party lives next to you or across the hall, and so on, just as if they were going to have a future in this building.

Why did I take that course of action? I wasn't certain of the right thing to do. I was at best a marginal and late player to the project. I could see "right" in a lot of places. The project did create gains. A blighted neighborhood got an anchor – a new housing complex which has continued to be an anchor, now mostly filled with residents who can afford to live there. The funders saw the agency as having pulled off a showpiece, enhancing the likelihood of landing more projects for this struggling city center. The developer, the agency, the attorney, and I all made money, the developer, as usual, making the most. He was the one person involved from the start who certainly should have known that the operating projections were presented in an overly favorable light – but then, operating projections always are. In most cases, the residents will ultimately pay the difference because they love the living space. In this case, the very low-income residents had no capacity to do so for themselves, and the outside funder had not signed on to subsidize them over the long term. The developer's job, strictly speaking, did not include protecting the residents; that fell to the agency, the lawyer, and the residents themselves.

There was at least one profound, agonizing loss. At the outset of the project the original players could have agreed, anticipating that matters would go awry, as they always do at some point, to hold the interests of the residents at least equal to everyone else's in working through problems. That never happened. When things began to go bad, those of us involved at that point had another opportunity to make that commitment. Again, it didn't happen. As a result, and without ever having a meeting about it or saying explicitly what we were doing, we final players left each very low-income family, individually and on their own, to reach the conclusion that they had failed to make a go of the most beautiful home they had ever owned.

In a previous chapter Art offered an explanation of why such choices get made. If a person or group is put into play, it's because of a weakness of some sort. A great weakness for very low-income people is having little to offer that's valued by the culture of success. That made it easy, in this case, for the residents to become the "moveable piece," for their interests to become the easiest element to put into play in reaching a solution.

When matters go awry in your professional life, whose interests are usually protected first? What form does "covering your ass" behavior take? Whose interests usually come last and are the easiest to sacrifice? What might be the implications for you and the projects you care about, in terms of your relative power in the system?

Summing Up

Using money as a tool to create different or better outcomes, even when the players are well-intentioned people with certain skills, is very, very hard. There is no cheap grace to be had dealing with the "right, wrong, and relative" of money. The phrase "cheap grace" comes from the work of Dietrich Bonhoeffer, a theologian active in the 1944 plot to assassinate Hitler. Ultimately, Bonhoeffer was hanged as part of Hitler's reprisal for the failed attempt on his life. Bonhoeffer, who came from a wealthy family, did not write about money and success. He witnessed and wrote about the proactive human capacity to resist evil. His thinking does strike an important chord for the issues of this book. There is no cheap or easy way to manage the seductiveness of money and the opportunities money promises. There are no clear markers through the ethical tangle of decision points that usually wind up, in the end, favoring some interests over others.

There are only three dead-honest questions to ask ourselves as we try:

Have you used money in ways that seem truly good? Can you do more in that vein?

What uses of money are clearly wrong in your eyes? Have you taken any actions that need to be unwound?

What actions have you taken that seemed relative, where you simply didn't know the right thing to do? In the light of experiences you've had since and wisdom you've gained, what can you do differently going forward?

The "right, wrong, and relative" of money comes roaring front and center when we integrate money into our daily lives. Because the promise of money is so seductive, we need a framework – one that evolves in sophistication as we go through life – for grappling with daily decisions. That framework can be one of fixed moral truths, as is taught by some religions, or, the framework can evolve in the form of agreed-upon norms that extend to embrace all of us.

CHAPTER EIGHT

"How Much Is Enough?"

"How much is enough?" is our final, integrating question – the one toward which the other questions of power, roles, purpose, and "framework for decision-making" all lead. In some ways "How much is enough?" is the most concrete and tangible, and in other ways the most philosophical and abstract, of money's hardest questions. This question plays itself out on multiple levels, each a familiar part of our human experience.

Here's one experience that served as a trigger for raising the question. Two founders of a software solutions company began a conference call with me, their voices ringing with elation. They had been approached with a possibility of selling the firm and cashing out. They were eager to pursue the sale and have the freedom to walk away from their long, demanding days. The third founder, also on the call, was upset and agitated. She declared her clear preference for retaining control of the company over the long term, even if that meant that real wealth would come to the three of them over time instead of in a lump sum.

As founders and consultant, we had worked together on the rapid growth of their company for several years. My response to this new opportunity was blunt. "Before you continue any conversation with the prospective buyer," I insisted, "before any offer is on the table, I want you each to decide how much money is enough to warrant your putting your relationship as owners in play. Once a big pile of cash is in front of your eyes, you'll be too dazzled to deal with the differences among you over the possible sale, and somebody's concerns will get trampled."

By "how much is enough?" I mean the amount that will allow you to stop driving so hard professionally should you choose to do so. I mean the amount that will allow you to feel safe, the amount that will compensate for risking hard-won relationships, the amount that will affirm your feeling good, smart, successful, accomplished, in control.

The question is deceptively simple. The answer is critical to integrating money with other aspects of your life and finding happiness. Of all the difficult questions about money, I see "How much is enough?" as the hardest, for several reasons:

"How much is enough?" leads you to ponder the really big philosophical questions, such as "what does it take, in real numbers, to be able to say I've made a difference, left a big footprint on the world?"

"How much is enough?" also leads you to big practical questions, like "How much creature comfort do I require in order to feel content?"

Your struggle over "How much is enough?" can become so consuming it can reach decisions about life and death.

A Very Knotty Question

The simple question, "How much is enough?" is a tangle of interlocking threads. One part of the story is almost always about money itself. Andrea came to see me because she felt caught in a bind. She wanted to continue with the work she loved, yet feared she would not have enough money to retire. At age 57, she had done church ministry all her life, never grossing more than $25,000 in salary. She had a tiny pension plan, few benefits, no savings, and considerable consumer debt. As we went more deeply into her story, she shared with me that her two young adult daughters had also chosen low-paying work. I asked if she had told them of her current dilemma, to allow them to learn from her experience and at least make their own career choices more intentional. She said she had not.

Another story thread can begin with a financial concern and quickly segue to the psychological issue of feeling safe in the world. When technology stocks tanked in early 2001, Patty lost a couple of million dollars – at least on paper. She was hit very hard emotionally by the loss. Her net worth remains in the seven-figure range, she is still working at a considerable salary, and she has a bright future, yet she doesn't feel safe and is worried about losing her entire net worth.

Another thread can be about the interplay between money and meaning. Karen, Michele, Anna, and Gisele, are nurse managers in a long-term care facility. Each is responsible for a unit that is home to forty medically frail, elderly residents. The nurse managers also coordinate the smooth operation of the unit so that doctors, medical residents, staff nurses, social workers, therapeutic recreation workers, dietary specialists, housekeepers, and a host of others can do their work. Nurse managers make in the mid-forties in terms of salary, and have a decent benefits package. These nurse managers have between eight and twenty-five years of experience. Their time is spent on day-to-day interactions with residents, staff, and families, and on supervising and documenting complex clinical care. They also support residents and families in crisis and at the moment of death. I asked these nurse managers if what they earn is enough, relative to the level of responsibility they face every day. They responded in unison. "If you went into it just for the money, you'd be sorely disappointed. You have to care about people, and get a lot of satisfaction out of helping people."

Yet another thread can be about professional standing, about reaching a level of success and being secure in knowing you've reached it. Sharon is 42 and president of a now highly profitable advertising agency under the wing of an international network. "Highly profitable" was not always the case. In 1996, the agency was losing accounts, bleeding money, and on the verge of going under. Recruited to spearhead the turnaround, Sharon completely re-vamped the senior leadership team, reworked the vision, took on the responsibility of new business development, and oversaw client accounts until experienced account managers could be hired. She worked killer hours, juggled the raising of two young children while maintaining a marriage, and ultimately prevailed. For that she is well-paid, earning a hefty six-figure salary, a bonus, stock options, and high professional visibility within her industry and in the community. During our interview she told me, "I've been on a very fast track all of my career. I always thought I got where I am because somebody else was a big part of my success. I gave myself credit, but always thought that if I hadn't had the support and help I wouldn't have succeeded. In those days I had to prove myself over and over again to whoever had been behind me. We had a make-or-break year for the agency in 1999. Because of the demands of the turnaround and some of the network politics, I ran the year completely by myself. What I didn't know I figured out, especially about the finances. Mastering the financial operations was really key. When I was really successful and turned a big profit and corporate still beat me up, I knew I couldn't jump any higher. I had done enough, and more than enough. There weren't many people who could have accomplished what I did. That was a real turning point for me. I understood that the person I had to prove things to was myself."

"How much is enough?" can have a deeply spiritual thread. Korean-born Steve is a physician, age 40. His brother is also a physician, as was his grandfather. Steve's late father, whom he admires and loves, was an engineer. His mother was college-educated, and brought Steve and his brother to the United States when Steve was in the eighth grade. His father remained in Korea to continue earning money while the rest of the family settled in Chicago, hooked up with the Korean Church, and learned the ropes in their chosen "land of opportunity."

Steve's father was a major influence in Steve's decision to become a physician. In his earlier years, the older man was ranked number 1 academically in his entire province in Korea. Because of that, he was sent to an MIT-equivalent university to become an engineer, because the country needed its brightest young men to help it reindustrialize after the devastation of the Korean War. All the smartest people were sent to the technical school. Steve laughs as he remembers what his father had told him. "All his dumb friends who went into medicine wound up living a higher life style." Steve's father drilled into his son that working for someone else for a salary was not desirable. Economic independence is the result of one sheet of paper – a diploma. "If you're going to go to school and earn a diploma, get one where you will make the best living."

The recent death of his father led Steve to ask "How much is enough?" in a spiritual sense as he struggled with the meaning of his father's life and his own. Steve is no longer religiously observant. He came to terms with his father's death, and with his own mortality, with this poignant reflection:

> Your father dies. He's an important person in your life. But the world goes on; it doesn't care. It doesn't miss a beat. Although I understand that intellectually, I felt the sun should stop shining for a moment to pay respect for his life. Instead, life just kept on as always.
>
> Life is insignificant. Your life is significant only to those around you for whom you are important. In the grand scheme of things, any one life is meaningless in a way.
>
> It makes you a little sad. You wish your life was a little bigger and more meaningful.

Finally, "How much is enough?" can become a profoundly existential question about living and dying itself. The provost of a major university system came to me for help in managing his crushing workload and resultant feelings of burnout. He was absolutely convinced that his performance on the job – no matter how many hours he put in – was far from good enough. Nor was his $200,000 a year salary enough. A closeted consumer, he was constantly buying and stashing away large-ticket items that his long work week gave him little time to use. He was experiencing serious physical consequences from his job stress: high blood pressure, migraine headaches, and mood swings that drove him to days of sleepless hyperactivity, then to the deepest despair and lethargy. His marriage was profoundly affected. After several appointments, he revealed the depths of his despair. He was actively considering suicide – not that day, not tomorrow, but soon, if his pain could not be alleviated.

After his first appointment, I had raised the possibility of him seeing a therapist in addition to our work. He had adamantly refused, citing the risk to him professionally should it become known that he was seeing "a shrink." Now I made the recommendation a must, explaining that I was not professionally trained to help him manage suicidal thoughts. I also told him that, although I cared about him, I couldn't collude with his dangerous teetering on the edge of ending his life. Angrily, and with great resistance, he accepted a referral. He made it as far as the therapist's office, then fled moments before his appointment was to have begun. He would not return my calls or the calls of the therapist trying to reschedule. Sadly, our work ended in that void.

The Financial Thread

"How much is enough" almost always ties together these financial, psychological, professional, spiritual, and existential threads. The easiest thread to deal with – perhaps surprisingly – is the financial. There are reliable and time-tested models available from financial service providers, accountants, in commercial software packages, and on the Web that will help you calculate the amount of money needed in order to maintain your lifestyle over the long term. "Maintaining your lifestyle over the long term" is what it means, in strictly financial terms, to know "How much is enough?" Those models typically take into account at least the following factors:

your age

your current asset base

the amount you can save over a period of time

historical data on rates of return for the assets you hold or will acquire

your current consumption patterns

your expectations for increased costs in retirement [as in the case of someone who anticipates extended travel]

the amount you wish to leave to heirs

any special needs for which you feel you must make provisions

With those data in hand, you can see what you'd have to do to achieve the goal of having income from capital – your savings and investments – replace income from earnings. That's the standard definition of financial independence, of "having enough." At first blush, what you'd have to do may seem completely out of reach. After a conference session at which I spoke, a participant who said he makes approximately $60,000 a year approached me. He said he was single, had no consumer debt to speak of, saved modestly in his company retirement plan, but couldn't see how he could squeeze another nickel out of his monthly budget toward the goal of investing. He, like Andrea with her commitment to church work, was doing work he loved. He didn't want to consider a change to a better-paying career, or change his lifestyle to reflect a more modest level of spending.

"Having income from capital replace income from earnings" is the standard definition of "having enough." You have the power to create your own definition, composed of the elements you can best live with. "Doing work you love" may be a big part of that definition. Being willing to work after you formally retire from your profession in order to supplement your pension and Social Security may be another part. Being willing to live with ongoing financial hardship as the price of staying where you feel professionally called can be a third.

What none of us gets to do safely is assume we have a "pass" on the need to address the issue of "enough." One of the most painful professional conversations I have is with men and women who have always worked for low wages, often in helping professions, or with women who get dumped after a life of being a homemaker, who say, "But I've given to others all my life – why am I having it so hard financially now? It isn't fair."

Whether you're going for the traditional definition or one of your own making, you can hire a financial advisor to help you make the most of your money, or you can create and execute something yourself. In either case, you'll be following these steps:

Define the level of your financial need, using what you spend now as a starting point.

Using mathematical projections, propose various scenarios to determine how much money invested, at what rate of return, will deliver the level of income you need.

Select a primary strategy, and subject that strategy to actual market simulations to determine the probability of success.

*Make a final decision about the strategy, and commit to the financial disci-
pline involved in implementing it.*

*Monitor the strategy and review the results. If your investments are not perform-
ing at a level that will achieve your financial objectives, make changes.*

In broad-brush strokes, that's the financial "how much is
enough?" information that's widely available from best-selling investment books, from investment houses, banks, and money managers,
from how-to investment videos and programs on television. However,
there's a much deeper level of understanding to be had, that has to
do with knowing what financially successful people know, and understanding how financially successful people act.

To get at that deeper level, I had a long and probing conversation
with my business partner, colleague, and husband of over thirty years,
Dr. Jeremy Klainer. In 1980 Jerry and I founded Professional Planning Corporation, an independent financial services firm that offers
fee-based investment advice, brokerage services, venture capital, and
real-estate development. For ten years I headed our brokerage division, about which you read in the previous chapter. One of our best
achievements was raising over $50 million to support the develop-
ment of low-income housing projects around the country. One of our
worst moments was "the damned dam." The $400,000 loss of which I
spoke early in the book was actually connected to the business. When
a clean-energy hydroelectric project for which we had raised money
from investors began to go bad, we stepped up personally to guarantee the financing so the investors wouldn't be hurt.

I left the financial services company in 1990 in order to undertake
the kind of consulting I do now. Jerry has stayed in the business, building and maintaining his money management relationship with clients
even as the markets do their convoluted dance. He and I have been
in and around the workings of money for most of our professional
lives, and conversations about money permeate our relationship.

Here's what we came up with as the most important principles
financially successful people know:

*There's a difference between income and capital, which is the difference
between "earning money" and "having money." * When I asked Steve and
Sharon to give me a number that represented "enough" to allow them

to feel safe, both of them quoted a figure in the low millions of dollars. When I asked the nurse managers, they said "a year's salary in the bank." To achieve financial independence, to allow income from capital to replace income from working, you need to amass a sufficiently large pool of capital and have it wisely invested. A year's salary in the bank is a useful financial cushion, but not a path to financial independence.

Your capacity to generate earnings will be enhanced if your product or service is scalable. That is, can you use the same concept more than once? Can you find a way to be compensated that doesn't depend on a limited resource, like the number of hours you can work? As Steve's father pointed out to him, being a wage earner from 8 A.M. to 5 P.M. offers no option for scalability. Both McDonald's and Starbucks offer examples of concepts that are scalable. They use a simple, well-defined business model over and over and over. You can get the same quality hamburger or cup of coffee where I live, where you live, when you travel, when you get stuck at an airport, or when you visit a food court in a classy hotel in Las Vegas. Sharon's creative work, by contrast, is not scalable. Her agency has to come up with an innovative and unique advertising campaign for each client. You'll have an easier time achieving financial independence if you can figure out a way to earn money, then let the concept go out and make money without you.

The chance to build capital is enhanced if your product or service can become the standard in an area where there are high barriers to entry and high costs to change. On an individual level, "high barriers to entry" can mean a long and rigorous training, such as was undertaken by my pediatric oncologist friend. Physicians in demanding medical specialties – especially those at the cutting edge of establishing advanced treatment protocols – make a lot of money because it's hard to become what they are. On a corporate level, the obvious example is Microsoft Windows, which became almost the universal operating system that drives software for personal computers. Microsoft has some competitors, but developing an operating system is an expensive research and development project, and gaining market share against Microsoft is a formidable undertaking. If almost everyone in the world uses Microsoft, it's just easier and more efficient for a new computer user to plug into Microsoft too. If you could own Microsoft, or own an alternative operating system that's highly innovative but has no market share, in which position would you rather be?

Within a product or service category, you're ahead of the game if you understand what determines "worth." Understanding worth allows you to determine pricing. Watches, for example, have a perceived worth that is more than their function of telling time. Inexpensive electronic watches actually keep time more accurately than certain more expensive models that have complex internal movements and are likely to lose three or four minutes a month. Yet an expensive brand has far greater worth to the wearer than a cheaper, although more accurate, brand. Similarly, you may have a job title that legions of other people also hold. What makes what you do worth more?

You also have an edge if you understand what determines value in our culture, which is largely based on "degree of uniqueness" and "degree of scarcity." People often comment on the seeming absurdity of paying Tiger Woods millions in tournament prize money to hit a ball into a cup, or paying Mia Hamm millions in endorsement fees because she can kick soccer goals. We all know people who do far more socially redeeming things that earn them a pittance. The high payback happens because the level of athletic giftedness demonstrated by these two people is both unique and scarce. Hardly anyone else can do what they do so well, so consistently, under such varied conditions, and over a long period of time. By contrast, the skills involved in providing personal care to the frail elderly – washing, dressing, feeding – can be taught within a short time to anyone who has reasonable intelligence and an average amount of human empathy. If you want to gain traditional financial independence, figure out what you can do that's unique and scarce, and focus your career choices there.

How much of that did you know when you started your career? How much is enough to know now, if you want to end up a financially successful person? You need to know – or at least consider – all of it.

Acting on Financial Wisdom

Your learning curve about money can be enhanced if you master what financially successful people already know. Your career trajectory can be greatly accelerated if you act like professionally successful people act.

Successful people tend to be high energy, restless, and competitive. On graduating from medical school, Steve had to apply to a residency program. His acceptance into a residency would determine his advanced medical training and the kind of medicine he would practice. What was the defining factor in his choice? "I applied to the residency program that was, by definition, the hardest one to get into. You wanted to try for it, just because it was so hard. That was probably the biggest factor in my choice." Programs that are hard to get into create a scarcity of that particular talent and training; not everyone can get in. Scarcity creates economic value. Steve's compensation as a physician is well at the high end of medical specialties.

Successful people are resilient and thick-skinned. Often they voluntarily choose the harder path with its complications and challenges, as if to flex that capacity to overcome obstacles and bounce back from adversity. That way, when business circumstances turn challenging, they have lots of reserve strength to draw upon. Sharon could have easily stayed at the large ad agency where she had worked prior to the turnaround offer, risen through the ranks and been well-compensated. Instead, she voluntarily sought the ups and downs of what she knew would be a very difficult transformation. Early in that process she was vilified by a local business reporter, who portrayed her as a cold and calculating leader willing to push longtime employees aside in the interests of her own ambition. The characterization hurt but did not deter Sharon's painstaking progress in getting the right people in place to save the agency. Years later, the transformation complete, Sharon sought coverage of the opening of a spectacular new office space. The reporter showed little inclination to return for another look. Sharon's response was clear and forceful. "This time, when that writer didn't want to come back, I made it happen. I used the power of my connections in a way that I thought was appropriate for the repositioning of the company." Being resilient in response to what people think of you is valuable. Knowing how to exert positional power in a way that makes the right things happen is also valuable.

Successful people assume they will prevail, even in the face of daunting challenges. They know failure is a theoretical possibility, but waste little time and energy considering that it might be a possibility for them. All their energy, adroitness, creativity, and adeptness are focused on moving forward. As one CEO leading a turnaround said, "I knew if I was going to go down, I would go down on my own merits. I knew I would leave no stone unturned, and I knew I wouldn't quit – even after I discovered things were much worse than the board of directors had revealed during the interview process."

Successful people take it as a given that they will perform the level of work needed to get where they want to go. One of my clients accepted a three-week rush contract that would vault her young company several levels higher in terms of the competition. To fulfill the requirements, she worked in her office during the day, and then went home to have supper with her husband and two toddlers. After putting the children to bed, she spent most of the night on her laptop working on the project, slept for couple of hours, showered and dressed while her husband got the children up and dressed, sat down and had breakfast with everyone, kissed everyone good-bye as her husband loaded the children in the car for a trip to day care, and went back to her office. In three weeks the project was completed, her family life had stayed reasonably intact, and the rest of her deliverables for other clients remained largely on schedule. Catching up with her sleep took several weeks, but there seemed to be no visible negative consequences other than that.

The things successful people don't do very well are: hang around, relax, or play. Successful people don't very often ramble down leafy paths; they run marathons or competitive road races. They don't go out to bat a few tennis balls around; they play well enough to be ranked, or they don't play. They don't ride around the neighborhood on fat-tire bikes with wide comfy seats; they have ultralight road bikes with special gel saddles on which they spend Saturdays touring or completing a "century" – 100 miles in a single day.

I use "they" when I speak of the behavior of successful people, when of course I mean "we." My Terry Classic road bike with its gel saddle is in the garage, waiting for me to jump on and head out of the city to ride thirty or forty miles along the rolling countryside. Jerry has been in a serious seven-day-a-week aerobic and weight training program. For his upcoming birthday, he plans to ride his bike across the United States.

The Psychological Thread

In puzzling over how much is enough from a psychological perspective, the people I work with tend to use two phrases: "enough to make me feel safe" and "enough to let me feel in control." Often, as in Patty's case, "enough" starts with a financial event but quickly shifts beyond money. Despite her millions in paper losses, Patty still has a seven-figure-net-worth, with the reasonable expectation of much more to come over her working lifetime. That, by any objective standards, is "enough." Over a fifty-year window, a diversified stock portfolio has averaged a rate of return of approximately 10% – much higher in some years, and lower in others. Given her net worth, Patty could reconfigure her portfolio to deliver income and expect to receive some hundreds of thousands of dollars a year. That's enough money to live on, even in the pricey urban center where she lives, but not enough for her in terms of "safety." She describes her longing for safety in this way:

> Feeling safe in the world is my core issue. Maybe it means having people in my life that I can count on. I'm surprised the money doesn't make me feel safer. I really thought it would. In some ways money highlights the things you thought being successful was going to fix. When that doesn't happen, you have a big 'aha' moment. If you don't deal with your inner stuff, having money doesn't make you feel safe either.

Like many successful people, Patty no longer practices the religion of her childhood. In my experience, people with an active religious practice close the "safety" gap with the belief that God will not forget them. Some of my elderly in-laws are Orthodox Jews whose daily religious observance is a reminder to them and to the world that God is always attentive to the faithful, and they are always attentive to God. One of the elderly professors who taught me philosophy at the College of St. Elizabeth is now in a nursing home. She has lost her mobility and her contact with students, her world of books and ideas, and the intellectual life of a college campus. From her small room she sends me notes that read "The Light of God Brightens our Days." I know how much she means that in her life and how fervently she wishes it were true in mine. When I taught stewardship studies at our local divinity school, the adult students were constantly saying things like "God has a plan for me; nothing happens by chance," and "I know God will never test me beyond my ability to cope." I suspect readers of this book with an active religious faith don't think so much about money as a way to achieve safety. They worry instead about using money to be good enough servants, good disciples, and faithful stewards.

The rest of us are left with some variation of the existentialist philosophy that so focused my attention as a college student in the 1960s. The College of St. Elizabeth in Convent Station, New Jersey, was an unlikely place to be drawn to the writings of Camus, Sartre, and their fellows; the standard curriculum featured the more traditional writings of St. Thomas Aquinas, Plato, and Aristotle. As a philosophy major I had to complete all of those courses. Then, responding to my insistence, the chair of the department agreed to an independent study. She and I sat across from each other in her office, arguing the merits of Camus' belief that, in a world without ultimate meaning, humans have to create their own meaning by choosing to live as if life were safe and as if life matters. I remember this deeply religious woman gripping the sides of her desk until her knuckles were white, fixing me with an intense glare that I always returned in equal measure. We students didn't know personal details about the nuns' lives back then. I have no idea to this day whether Sister Frances suffered from something physical that caused her to grip the desk in pain, or whether the pain came from this smoldering intellectual struggle that was so alien to her own beliefs and values. Oddly enough, her willingness to engage with me around the idea that as human beings we must create meaning in the world – about our money, our life purpose, and our relationships – was a great gift, although I'm sure not the one she intended.

If the "safety gap" is not closed via religious beliefs or an existential worldview, we can also look to the insights of psychology. Dr. Mary Jane Herron is a psychotherapist in private practice. Herron describes the sense of psychological safety with regard to money as "the removal of the threat of disruptive dangers as well as the ability to acquire more than basic necessities. A 'safe money place,' where one can rest easy and feel grounded, is where you have what you want, and what you don't have you don't seek."

Karen Mackie is a therapist and a dancer. For her, "safe" and "unsafe" are primary experiences we grasp in our bodies:

There is a tale attributed to Buddha:

Buddha was giving a talk to a group of disciples while holding a bird in his palm. The students were fascinated by Buddha's ability to prevent the bird from flying away and were unable to duplicate his feat. Finally, unable to restrain their curiosity, they asked "Master, why does the bird not fly away?" The Buddha responded: "It is quite simple, my friends. Each time I sense the bird will take flight, I simply drop my hand a bit and the bird has nothing to push off from."

I think this is a great "body story" of the felt experience of "unsafe." A sense of psychological safety is the platform from which each of us pushes off into the world. Without that sense, people feel anxious, alone, and unsure. A child unsure of the messages being received from anxious or inattentive parents has no platform, and consequently has difficulty creating a sense of self. The adult who emerges from this beginning is often plagued by self-doubt internally but outwardly fits in to whatever is required by the social environment.

If parents don't literally and metaphorically provide a "steady hand" then much internal energy tends to be spent later in life trying to find something that will "hold" reliably – work, religion, relationships, etc. Fortunately, some of those systems do work well enough so that one is not "doomed" by the experience of a flimsy or shaky parental start in life.

The Professional Thread

During the early years of her career, Sharon jumped through endless hoops established by others to prove she was delivering enough, that she was good enough. Now, at 42, she picks her own challenges, negotiates appropriate financial rewards, and has clearly internalized her own standard of what it means to do "great work." That means Sharon has internalized the difference between "validation" and "affirmation" when she asks herself how much is enough.

People who are dependent on validation constantly seek external recognition – usually from people who have more power than they do – for their accomplishments. That recognition takes forms like a salary increase, an award, a seat at the honorary "president's leadership council." Without external recognition, people who wait for validation really have no reliable sense of whether or not what they do is any good. The idea that you could deliver great work and still not be recognized or chosen is alien to them. If no one in a position of power thinks what you do is good enough to win recognition, how can your work be good?

The most insidious part of working for validation is that "my deliverables weren't good enough" quickly becomes "I'm not good enough." Since external validation is always fleeting – what you proved to someone today is exactly what you'll have to prove again tomorrow – waiting for validation is a surefire recipe for burnout.

"Affirmation" is different. "Affirmation" sounds like this: "I'm sure what delivers value in my industry. It's nice for other people to recognize me as valuable and say so in some way. Whether or not they do, I know when I'm doing great work. My confidence in that and in myself isn't shaken just because no one else stands up and salutes."

"Affirmation" has a hook to it. "Whether or not other people recognize my good work" doesn't mean standing around and waiting for people to give you raises or promotions. I've counseled numerous talented people at all career stages who have delivered consistently fine work over a significant period, then were unexpectedly passed over for the promotion that was surely "theirs." They usually feel shocked, angry, and betrayed. "I don't get it. After all I've given to this organization, how much more do I have to do to show that I'm good enough?"

Understanding what delivers "value" in your particular setting, and trusting that you know when you've created value, carries with it an obligation. We live and work in a noisy culture where all of us, including bosses, have multiple demands on our time and attention. If you want someone to notice your good work and pay or promote you accordingly, you need to develop a compelling and continual story that will grab attention. That "tooting your own horn" may or may not come naturally to you. A client of mine was raised in a Mennonite household where modesty and humility were paramount values. Now the executive director of a large nonprofit agency responsible for building community coalitions, she is involved in turf wars all the time. She's had to learn to publicly proclaim her experience, judgment, and insight in order to win a fair share of grant resources for her agency.

How do you move from seeking validation to enjoying affirmation, while anchoring yourself in your internal understanding of "enough"? There are several ways:

Recognize the turning point for Sharon. Remember what Sharon finally understood: "When I was really successful and turned a big profit and corporate still beat me up, I knew I couldn't jump any higher. Not many people could do what I had done." Sometimes "really good work" is so clear, so obvious, that we simply can't subjugate our accomplishments to the approval of others. After years of experience in the ad industry and a huge effort to accomplish the turnaround, Sharon knew very well what she had done. Having corporate voluntarily come across with the appropriate financial recognition would have been nice. Anchored in her own certainty of the quality of the work and the turnaround, Sharon was well-positioned to insist on and receive enhancements to her contract.

Learn the business model that anchors your company or nonprofit, and commit to achieving that understanding regardless of where you sit in the organization. How is "worth" determined? With that understanding, you can be more successful at building the case for your own worth, and negotiating accordingly.

Get a grip and recognize how fleeting validation really is. How many managers have you worked for or clients have you tried to satisfy whose philosophy is "What have you done for me today"? The search for validation never ends. External validation can be a tremendous ego boost. It also isn't very good for you, because it's likely to distract you from your own sense of what's good and meaningful and make you focus on the performance hoops other people are holding out. Eating high-butterfat ice cream tastes wonderful in the moment. However, most of us have worked hard to reduce our craving for it because we now know it clogs up our arteries. Validation is like that. The ego hit is great, but the feedback has bad consequences. Instead of focusing on validation, try strengthening your own sense of what's "good enough." Your gain will be more enduring.

Spiritual Threads, and Life/Death Decisions

Steve is a little sad about the meaning of life, because he would like that meaning to be "a little bit bigger." The beleaguered provost, a caring and competent man, is so burdened by the thought that nothing he does is good enough that he thinks of ending his life.

How much is enough? How much do we have to earn, accomplish, work though, risk, believe in, and hope for to have it feel like enough? How much, and of what, will allow us to live a life that matters, and die at peace with ourselves and with the world?

Both Steve and the provost earn solid six-figure incomes. They have enough money. Both men enjoy the professional respect of their colleagues and those they serve. In terms of making a big footprint professionally, both have already accomplished that goal while still in their 40's. Steve has been in medical practice just over ten years. During that time, he and his partner have treated more than 30,000 patients, often providing much-needed and complex surgical procedures. The provost, on a daily basis, is involved in far-reaching decisions that affect the lives of tens of thousands of students, faculty, and staff. Both men have long-term marriages, which shows enough psychological well-being to sustain a least some close relationships. Steve is the father of three children, and a devoted son to the aging mother he now helps support.

What would it look like for the meaning of Steve's life to be a little bigger? What would it feel like for the provost to rest assured that digging as deeply as he does into his reserve of energy, intelligence, and experience is good enough?

Sometimes we find answers to the hardest questions in the least expected places – like a nursing home. I first came to know nurse managers Karen, Michele, Anna and Gisele, as part of a consulting project I accepted at the Jewish Home of Rochester, the long-term care facility where they work. Long-term care facilities, more commonly known as nursing homes, are far out of the mainstream in terms of the culture of success. Nothing moves fast. There's no running with the pack. As a medical specialty, geriatric care pays far less than other medical disciplines; the medical director at the nursing home makes hundreds of thousands of dollars less than a prominent cardiologist or orthopedic surgeon. Providing chronic care is a quiet specialty not usually associated with making a big and visible footprint on the world.

Nursing homes deliver at least two things of real value. They focus on alleviating the pain and suffering that are part of diseases and injuries common in the elderly, and they see to quality of life for people who can no longer live at home or be cared for by family. Diagnosing and prescribing treatments for disease and injury fall more to the doctors. Both ongoing clinical care and seeing to quality of life falls more to the nurses. Although geriatric facilities pay less well overall than acute-care settings, within this health facility the medical director is paid four or five times what the nurse managers are paid. To me that means, in a literal sense, that society values the management of disease and injury in older people four or five times more than we value a more integrated approach to their quality of life.

I suspect physical well-being is not alone at the very top of anyone's list when we try to articulate what it might look like for the meaning of life to be bigger. Being free of pain, illness, and injury is certainly on the list; those things are tremendously important, but I think they are not the most important, or at least not four or five times as important, as overall quality of our lives. Let me give an example.

One of the nurse managers, Michele, shared this story about one of her residents. The woman, who suffered from a complex and debilitating neurological condition, had a husband who was terminally ill and being cared for in a hospice nearby. On heavy morphine for pain and near death, he had expressed a longing for his wife, a strong desire to "see her face and kiss her" one last time. For a nurse manager to leave her unit and leave the facility for a couple of hours on short notice is no small feat. Health facilities these days are tightly staffed; there are fewer trained people to cover when someone is out. Nonetheless, Michele moved quickly, wanting to bring the two together while the husband was still conscious. She found coverage for the unit, arranged transportation, and accompanied the woman on this brief but emotionally difficult journey. Once at the hospice and with the help of hospice workers, Michele gently placed the woman in her husband's bed, closed the door, and left the two alone.

In private, husband and wife were able to share their good-byes. They had, for a last time, the simple warmth and comfort of each other's bodies. All those who waited outside the room sensed that the moment was enough, and would allow the man to die in peace. On the trip back to the nursing home, the woman told Michele the visit had "meant the world to me – more than I can say."

What Does the Story
Say about "Enough"?

"You can't put a price tag on empathy."

"You're comparing apples and oranges. How can you possibly rank the worth of keeping a dying cancer victim free of pain against the worth of giving the two a last opportunity to see each other?"

"We couldn't possibly decide on a moment-to-moment basis what the most worthwhile outcome might be and compensate people accordingly. We have to use criteria – like years of training and education and experience – that hold constant and create a marginal difference in most cases."

Those objections are all perfectly true. Some other realities are true as well.

We ask a lot of each other, and don't always give enough back. At 30, Michele is one of the youngest and most energetic nurse managers. Still, the emotional demands of the job weigh heavily on her. Some days she goes home too exhausted to have much of herself left over for her husband, whom she describes as "a very understanding guy." Between two salaries they make a good living, but not a robust one. They forgo things such as cleaning services that would lighten Michele's job of running her own household and help her with stress. One of the other nurse managers, Karen, has an even more acute concern. She has just been diagnosed with a recurrence of breast cancer. As she prepares herself and her family for the ordeal of a double mastectomy, she has another set of tasks. She must negotiate a three-month hiatus on her mortgage, her car payment, and her credit card bills. While working, she makes $900 a week. For the period of her recovery, her employer-based disability will pay her $175 a week, and ends simply will not meet. When she returns to work, her own physical and psychological healing still underway, she will have to return full tilt to paying the bills and being the emotional center of her unit. You can't place a price tag on empathy, but we make life financially hard for the people we rely on to provide it.

We intuitively know that some people do work that is worth a great deal, while others in the same job category put out barely enough to keep their jobs. We just don't know how to express that differentiation in pay, so we use other measures, such as number of degrees and years on the job. That means you can have a much less talented person making far more on the pay scale than a more talented and effective worker who hasn't had the time or wherewithal to obtain extra credentials. When we think about that, it makes no sense – so we mostly avoid thinking about it.

Finally, on the topic of comparing apples and oranges, it is hard to assess the relative worth of various kinds of work across professional disciplines. In my view, the questions should still be asked and answered – that's the whole untapped organizational layer of being serious about "how much is enough?"

"Enough," whether raised as a personal issue or a matter of organizational effectiveness, is always a question of relative worth. In the simplest sense, "enough" is having what matters most to you last as long as you need it.

Having enough money matters. Having money during your lifetime will gain you choices. Having money toward the end of life will gain you access to supportive care at home, or to a bed in a private nursing home. Once there, your care will be the same as the person in the next bed, who's on Medicaid. Neither of you will need much spending money. What money buys – containers to hold your expectations – you don't need any more. What you do need – a fresh lease on life – money can't buy. So, money is part of "enough," but fails to meet all the criteria.

Feeling safe enough or in control enough matters also. Feeling safe during your lifetime gives you the stability and confidence to take bigger risks. At the end of life, we all stand poised at the edge of the least-understood human experience: death. Most of us don't feel either safe or in control about going toward an event no one knows anything about, so safety and control matter more during life than at life's end. Again, they're part of "enough" but fail the "last as long as you need it" test.

Professional success matters. Having professional success during your lifetime is a big ego boost, and gives you challenging problems around which to stretch your intelligence and creativity. Like feeling safe and in control, professional success matters much less at the end of life. We may not get to keep our success intact. In *Elegy for Iris*, British author Iris Murdoch's husband John Bayley wrote a touching tribute to her life and to their life together. He also talked about his quiet anguish at watching her once-brilliant mind succumb to Alzheimer's disease. No longer able to read a page of what she had once written, his beloved Iris spent the last years of her life in front of the television being amused by cartoons. The professional success for which we drive ourselves to the point of exhaustion is part of "enough," but not all.

Spiritual wholeness – the ability to let your spirit go where it needs to go – matters hugely, both during life and at life's end. Many of us, especially those who want to run at the front of the pack, spend a lot of time and energy doing what we ought to do, and fleeing from what we most long for. It shouldn't take being terminally ill to allow us the comfort of another human being coming close. That doesn't necessarily mean marriage; finding a spouse or partner doesn't happen for everyone. It does mean intimacy. Intimacy means being there – not having to be witty or funny or brilliant or successful or rich or "on." Intimacy is just being fully present, and allowing someone to be fully present to you. With people in our lives whose simple presence makes us feel better, most of us have the courage to live a life that matters and die a peaceful death. For me, that's the one experience that both matters and can last as long as we need it. Spiritual wholeness gives a big and profound meaning to life – and it's enough.

While you're working on money and success, you need to put at least that much effort into developing relationships with people who make you feel better just by being around. That's the one thing that can last all the way to the end. If you don't have such relationships, you'll probably never feel as if you have enough – no matter your level of financial success, or how big a footprint you make on the world.

CHAPTER NINE

"Don't Just Talk about Money and Happiness – Reach for It!"

MONEY IS NOT ONLY a unique and revealing window showing us who we really are. Money is also a powerful tool for changing our lives. If you're like most of us, money works better for you in some ways than in others. You can change your money story – and thereby your life – with the goal of feeling more powerful, gaining more meaning from your day-to-day experience, and better recognizing happiness. To do that, you not only have to understand the roots of your money story and think differently about money in the present. You have to act differently going forward. As you come to believe and act differently, over time you can reshape who you are. That's what "harnessing the power of money" really means. The ability to keep changing, keep growing, is the real benefit of what I call "walking the talk" on money.

People in circumstances you'll be able to recognize have been able to change their relationship with money and success and find a much deeper level of happiness. That possibility exists for you as well. As has been true with each chapter, what's important here is not to critique or affirm how well someone else has reconfigured a life. What's important is for you to see several models of how it's possible to do so. You then have some guideposts for creating change on your own.

Jumping In

When Lynn and I first met she was 36 and had recently given birth to her second child, a daughter then three months old. Lynn was preparing to return to her three-day-a-week director of marketing position for a regional health plan. The plan is a major player among corporate health insurers, covering two million people and generating $2 billion in revenue. Lynn was very, very eager to get back to work. Married for twelve years to a man content with a mid-level management role in a small company, Lynn feared that her return to work would reignite their previous provider/organizer tensions. With great frustration she told me, "I work harder than my husband, earn more money, and am more ambitious. When I'm back at work, I don't want to be still up at midnight folding his underwear."

Lynn's decision to work three days a week after the birth of her first child "was driven by a desire to experience what it was like to be a mother at home with a child. With the hours I had been working, I just felt like I was only experiencing a small piece of motherhood. My own mom had stayed at home. She had four children and ran the house; my dad had his own business. When I came home, she was always there with baked goods. That was a very powerful image. It certainly added to the guilt that someone else was in my house making cookies for my son."

During her period of part-time work Lynn did get labeled as being "on the mommy track," although the more senior executives who had been her champions always assumed it to be a temporary situation. She lost some political ground in the company, but "not as much as you would think. I'd been here long enough to make good decisions about when to be visible and when I could risk being away – which I couldn't have done as astutely if I'd been new. One of my mentors also saw to it that I got the right projects to work on. If there are two or three projects in a year that make a key difference for any company, he made sure those were the kinds of projects I was given."

Lynn also discovered important things about herself as a full-time mother.

At first the novelty was wonderful. Here it was, 10 A.M. on a Monday morning, and I was at the bagel shop with my 2-year-old having bagels with a Mom's coffee group. My stress level was much lower; the biggest problem I had was what snack to put into the diaper bag. My being at home did cause some role problems in my marriage. I felt that if I was there all day, I should pick up the dry cleaning and have dinner on the table when my husband got home. I really resented it. That was a hard period in our marriage. I realized I was bored, low energy, close to being depressed. I felt like I was missing something back on the career side.

When Lynn did return to work, now with two young children at home, she was offered a significant promotion: elevation to corporate vice-president of marketing, with responsibilities across the entire region. She would get a considerably enhanced salary and benefits package, taking her into the mid-six figures. She would get a regular seat at the table, grappling with policy and strategic decisions that shaped the future of her company – not as an organizer or project manager charged with carrying out decisions, but as a decision maker herself. That, as Lynn recognized, is "real power. And you don't get that when you're at home with a four-year-old and an infant." Having real power is also consistent with Lynn's longer-term vision for herself, which is to be a health care CEO. An expectation, pointedly conveyed several times during the job negotiation, went along with the offer. Lynn would give up the three-day-a-week schedule she had maintained with her first child and return to work full-time.

After careful consideration of the expected gains and losses, Lynn accepted the whole package.

It took me a long time to admit that I was very ambitious. The most important truth for me to recognize has been that I am more ambitious than my husband, and that's OK. This is who I need to be. It took my husband more time to figure out what he personally gains from my being ambitious. He gets children who can go to a private school that he could never send them to on his income. He gets a new car. He gets a wife who's very happy. He gets financial stability. It was incredibly stressful for him to think he had to be the primary breadwinner.

Part of the conversation between Lynn and her husband during this period was his acknowledgment that he had also been offered a big promotion and raise, but didn't want it. That pushed Lynn to do some work with me around her expectations of her husband and his career. Initially, she had questioned his seemingly "subdued" ambition. Through our conversation, she acknowledged that giving their children the attention they needed would be much harder if both she and her husband were on an accelerated career track. Consciously or unconsciously, Lynn had chosen to marry a man she loved, but who also fit with her career ambitions. Recognizing and accepting their counterculture provider/organizer model, she was able to tell him, "Great. I don't need you to be an executive. It wouldn't work. One of us has to have some flexibility around the needs of the kids." Her husband is now the one consistently at home in the evening and available during the days for doctor appointments and emergencies.

There was another element to Lynn's being at peace with her own career choices and those of her husband. "He travels internationally as part of his job, and I really respect that. What works for us is that even though my husband doesn't work the hours I do and isn't at the same level, he's got something that I don't have but really respect – the opportunity to go abroad. He's got a basis for his own self-esteem, in a way that's not competitive with mine."

Although Lynn recognizes that having her husband and a nanny so heavily involved in the children's care is an outcome of her own choice, she is troubled about some aspects of life at home.

> I guess there are two kinds of guilt. One is admitting that I'm leaving the care of my children to someone else. My husband is a wonderful father, and the children have a lot of time with him. And, in the morning, I leave my children in their pajamas with a nanny that's snuggling with them and feeding them breakfast. I walk out the door at 7:30 A.M., and one of us won't walk in the door again until 5:30 or 6:00 at night. I do lose sleep over it, and pray I'm making the right decision. I really worry about it, although the kids seem perfectly happy. The other guilt was that I make enough money so I can have a full-time nanny. At first I used to call her "the babysitter." Then I had to acknowledge that her importance in our family support system far exceeds babysitting, and it wasn't fair to diminish her role. I had to give up my "superwoman" reputation at work and be honest about how much competent help it takes to be a mother of small children and a full-time senior executive.

Although her worry about the children is ongoing, Lynn is clear what she has gained by acknowledging her own ambition, and accepting the promotion.

> Money is a significant motivator for me. I work in the realm of policy and strategic decisions – I don't have a "product" that shows my worth. So, how much I get paid is my way of knowing that I'm valued and that my contribution to the company is validated. Also, money and position opened up a number of doors I never even anticipated when I was trying to get this job. Money, even more than the new job title, put me in a peer group, made me part of the club. Being paid this kind of money makes my fellow executives – and they are almost all men at this level – far more comfortable with me. On all counts, I'm very happy with the promotion. When I'm happy, my energy level is very high. When I'm not doing what I like, I get very angry.

The container Lynn has chosen – a high-powered corporate career – is amply fulfilling her expectations. The choice has also meant giving up a flexible work situation that would be the envy of many working mothers. Perhaps most challenging of all, Lynn's decision requires unflinchingly honesty on a number of points:

The intensity of her ambition.

The degree to which her sense of self-esteem is structured around money and external signals like title, scope of responsibility, etc., rather than "marching to an internal drummer."

The role children play in her life, and that loving her kids and loving being full- time "cookie mommy" do not have to be one and the same.

Her acceptance of "counterculture provider/organizer" as the model that suits her marriage and family life the best.

"Jumping in at a deeper level" is one path to changing your relationship with money and success in a way that can make your behavior more consistent with your deepest beliefs and values. That's the change that has worked best for Lynn. Accepting the promotion, and all that goes with it, has not made Lynn's life worry-free. Accepting the promotion means Lynn is happiest choosing to have more of the energy and creative thrust her professional life provides at the cost of some degree of concern about her children. She monitors that balance all the time. At this point she says, "I've given up experiences in my children's lives, but I don't feel that I've crossed the line and given up things I will regret later." Lynn also monitors the relationship with her husband, recognizing that their choice of the counterculture provider/organizer model can create strains between the two of them, with in-laws, and among their circle of friends. Her assessment for now is that "It's working for my husband and me, without a personal toll on our marriage. If anything, our marriage is stronger than ever because of the work we've gone through with each other in relation to my accepting the promotion."

The decision to jump in at a deeper level is not, for most of us, a solitary choice. Taking any major step like that challenges our skills at successfully negotiating change with the people we most care about.

Jumping Out

Ron is 48, has been happily married for twenty-five years, and is the father of three young adolescent daughters. In deciding to have children, Ron and his wife chose the traditional provider/organizer model as the financial structure for their family life. "We've learned from experience that if two parents both try to share full-time work, neither one is really an effective full-time worker because a professional or executive position requires a commitment and flexibility above and beyond normal predictable hours." Ron's wife is in a helping profession, where she's defined a niche that keeps work flowing her way as long and as much as she wants it. She is also, as Ron acknowledges, "willing to accept relatively low pay and absolutely no status."

Ron was riding the wave of a highly successful twenty-year career with a medium-size general practice law firm, moving from associate to partner to head of the corporate department, then being tapped for consideration as managing partner of the entire firm. With real gratitude to his colleagues for looking to him as a leader, Ron declined to be a candidate for the position because "I could not imagine how I could carry out that responsibility without absolutely giving up everything else that was important to me." Some time later, he astonished his in-house colleagues and the wider legal community by deciding to leave the firm entirely and going into practice on his own. He is clear that his choice had nothing to do with dissatisfaction with the law firm or with the practice of law.

> I had been very well treated at that firm, a very good group of people, a generally high-minded and humane group of people who tried to pick the high road on many, many issues. It was, of course, a profit-making organization in a tough industry with tough people – that's the way law firms are. But overall, I think they were people who took pride in doing the right thing and who were very generous toward me. I left people who were friends and had been very good to me. I left a successful organiza- tion. Although no one ever said it in so many words, I think the people I'd worked with felt stunned and rejected – I was the last person anyone ever expected to leave the firm.

"Jumping out," as Ron's situation illustrates, can be a choice to replace one container that's working fairly well with another that you think and hope will better fulfill your expectations. Ron went into sole practice – consciously giving up some of the visibility, profes- sional stature, and "big footprint" that comes with being part of a law firm – for two key reasons.

He wanted to spend more time with his daughters in a way that would not conflict with his commitments to his law partners. Ron was willing to have the risks and rewards of his "forays into the unknown" fall on himself and his family. He was not willing to put his law partners at risk because of his desire to tinker with the preferred model of practicing law.

He likes actually practicing law more than being a rainmaker. As Ron explains it, law firms have "finders, minders, and grinders. 'Finders' are the classic rainmakers, the people who bring in business. These are people who, if they're on an airplane, will not come off the flight with- out two or three new clients in tow. 'Minders' are the people who, given those new clients, will do a fine job of cultivating them and nurturing them and making them happy. 'Grinders' are the people who will sit in the library and do bang-up research, or go argue a motion, or write a will, or crunch numbers." Although highly successful as a rainmaker – and indeed now, in his own practice, Ron bears sole responsibility for bringing in business – he did not want to become "a point in a profit center building larger and larger empires of younger lawyers who would be doing the work for clients I would bring in."

For Ron, being a good father means more than being the primary financial provider. Parenting his daughters means keeping regular hours. It means being around a lot, and making some visible sacrifices on the business side to be able to be in places and do things that matter to his children, such as being soccer coach and committing to regular practices with the team. "A lot of it, though, is just being home at dinner and being around on the weekend and being able to do things spontaneously with the girls – help with homework, listen, or just kid around. Over the last couple of weeks my wife and I had a couple of moral issues having to do with the girls' attitudes that weren't going to go away and were going to take more than two minutes to resolve. We finally worked it out as a family over a period of about two weeks, and if I hadn't been there it wouldn't have happened in the same way. My wife had her role, and I had my role – it just took time with the girls, and work. Now they're back in a certain direction that's consistent with our family values. If we hadn't taken the time with them, they'd be going off in another direction entirely."

For Ron, being a good sole practitioner of business law means knowing his strengths and capitalizing on them on behalf of his clients. "I'm pretty self-reliant. I have my own opinions on things, and I was never one who shopped opinions all over the law firm. I'm a problem-solver, someone who can look at a slightly bigger picture than a lawyer who is just a technician – but it's important that I can do a competent technical job too. I try, as much as I can, to be responsive to clients and just recognize that I'm helping them work through difficult problems. That's a professional approach to the work. Many lawyers take a more social approach to their relationship with clients. I don't tend to socialize with clients. What I have to sell and to offer is really just the abilities and efforts of a good tradesman."

In looking at his decision overall, Ron reflects on a trailing emotion that came with moving into sole practice:

> When I look at the career path that it takes to become truly prominent, you really have to go out and build a visibility in the community that I just don't care to build. Sometimes I look over at the partner in a very large law firm who's made a name in whatever area and I think to myself, "Well, I could have been that partner." I'm not going to have that kind of

recognition in my life. But, I have to remember that everything else that I have gained was a trade-off for recognition. When I remember the career path and the difficult burdens and compromises that I would have had to accept in terms of fulfilling billable hour requirements and committee and administrative expectations at a law firm, I get off that longing for prominence very easily.

Money was part of the reason Ron originally chose law as his profession. As he recalls, "I'm not sure I deliberated all that consciously about it, but the idea of having a job where you're pretty well paid and have some professional stature seemed nice to me." Money is still important. "Financial success says something to me about achievement and recognition and all the other things. It wouldn't have been fine with me if going into sole practice meant a drastic reduction in what I was making. Fortunately, things have worked out, and that didn't happen."

As in Lynn's case, Ron had to look at four basic factors in making his decision to "jump out" of an expected career path. He had to consider the intensity of his ambition. He had to assess his need for external validation – the kind that comes with moving up the ranks in a law firm – as opposed to the internal sense of satisfaction that comes from capitalizing on one's professional strengths and satisfying the expectations of clients. He had to look at the role of children in his life and the relative importance of parenting. He had to look at the traditional provider/organizer model he and his wife had chosen as the basis of their family financial security and see if the model could withstand a dramatic change.

In addition, Ron's story brings to light two additional considerations.

Most of us need a secure platform from which to launch a dramatic change. Earlier in the book, Karen Mackie talked of a Buddhist fable in which a healthy bird needed a secure hand from which to take flight. That fable applies here as well. Part of Ron's secure platform was some degree of family money that he is slated to inherit. If his move into sole practice had been a disaster financially, there would still have been money to send the girls to college. If absolutely necessary, Ron could have approached his elderly parents and tapped that expected inheritance in order to fund another transition. An equally important part of the secure platform was the attitude of Ron's wife. "She made it possible for me to take risks by volunteering that she didn't care what we had to live on as long as I could be happy with what I did all day. She used to complain about my former long hours, not only for her own sake but because, in her view, I lost other opportunities for my time and abilities. Finally, I knew that whatever happened she would look forward and not second-guess my decisions. These are big things to someone poised before a consequential decision."

We need to be unflinchingly honest about how big a professional footprint we need to leave on the world in order to feel successful. The imprint of an individual law practice, as Ron himself acknowledges, is unlikely to be as large as the imprint of a major law firm with a national or a global reach, no matter how skilled and sophisticated the individual practitioner. This is the trade-off Ron reflected on when he spoke of prominence in the legal community, the cost of achieving it, and his own choice to be a successful lawyer without depriving his daughters of a father who's more likely than not to be around when they need him.

Jumping Sideways

Both Lynn and Ron had been thinking for some time about whether their highly successful work situations were in fact making them happy. In Lynn's case, the musing was brought to a decision point by an external event: the offer of a new position. Ron was pushed into action by two related factors: his daughters' move into adolescence and a stronger peer group affiliation, and the continued recognition that the demands of the law firm were precluding his spending as much time with them as he wanted.

What if you are successful at work, on a fast track, moving happily toward a very senior position that you want very much, and you hit a wall? In that case, the question of walking the talk comes after the fact, not before.

Arun is 58, the father of a grown son and daughter who are both working and live in other cities, a husband of thirty-two years, and, consistent with his culture of origin, a responsible provider for extended family both here and in India. "Responsible" means financially responsible and personally available. Arun travels back to India to see his relatives on a regular basis. He has helped family members financially, especially with educational needs. Education holds an immense value in the family. Arun's father made sure that not only his sons but also his daughters received a college education, which Arun remembers as "kind of unique in India at that time."

Arun came to the United States when he was 18 to go to college, and stayed. A brilliant strategic thinker, he has had a stellar thirty-four-year career with a global technology company now experiencing turbulent times. He enjoys a solid six-figure income, a seven-figure net worth, and a strong and loving relationship with his wife, who is an American citizen. She is active as a community volunteer, and the two have always made time, whether Arun is at home or traveling, to talk with each other and share moments of each other's day.

Arun is financially independent, has more than enough years of service to retire, and is not nearly ready to do so. His role model for continuing to work is his dad, who is 88, lives in India, and still goes to work six days a week. "My Dad keeps telling me he would die if he just went and sat at home – you've got to remain active." Arun's motivation in remaining with this particular company and helping it through its difficulties is partly financial. A significant portion of his net worth happens to be tied up in deferred compensation. Should turbulent times actually swamp the organization, much – although not all – of that deferred compensation could be lost. Part of the motivation is pride: this is the organization to which he has devoted his entire professional life, and he would not like to see the product of those efforts fall by the wayside. Arun's devotion to work is also personal: he likes to remain intellectually challenged by dealing with knotty problems and tackling new opportunities.

Arun's wide-ranging career actually began very slowly. "I didn't really understand how to get around in an American company. Coming from India, my communications skills were not great. Also, people coming from Asia had this idea of seniority and status. If you worked for someone you held him in high regard so it was very difficult to disagree or argue." After that slow first year, Arun got a staff position in finance – a coup for him, and a reflection of the company's allowing anyone to succeed who could do the work. "In those days it was difficult for non-white Asians even to get jobs, much less in finance. At that time I couldn't even get interviews at the other big companies in town, who only hired whites for staff positions." Within seven years Arun was at senior management levels, and three years later he became an officer of a division, serving as vice president of customer administration for the United States. Some years later, at the urging of the CEO, he then made the geographical move to corporate headquarters.

At headquarters Arun was thrown into the intense competition to become a corporate officer, which he was given to believe was a realistic career goal. The promotion did not come. Another candidate was appointed to the position toward which Arun's career had been heading. "It was the one time in my life I had a goal that did not materialize: becoming controller for the entire corporation." Arun took being passed over as a clear sign that his upward momentum at this company had stopped.

This is a critical point in large work systems: the pyramid has greatly narrowed, and there are more talented candidates for any one slot than there are slots to be filled. What happens to your feelings of success and happiness if you're used to being the one who prevails, but this time you don't, and there's no other "up" spot for you to go? One option is to change companies. Arun had opportunities to relocate and work for a different company, where his upward mobility might well have continued. Relocation would have disrupted his family life in ways he chose not to do. Balancing personal success and family happiness is, for Arun, an important value.

Another option is asking yourself: "If I can't have what I want, can I learn to be challenged by what I have?" This moment is usually a pivotal life point for high achievers. Even having to face the question can devastate their happiness and self-esteem.

Arun could, and did, ask himself that question – and find a satisfying answer. "Fortunately, the company gave me an opportunity to run operational jobs. That was another way to broaden myself. The last ten to twelve years has not been a new grade so much as new jobs, and they're a lot of fun." His expectation of "happiness" has shifted from one container to another. Instead of "becoming the controller," Arun's expectations for fulfillment are now structured around the goal of "keeping myself continually challenged" – even if that means moving around laterally instead of moving up.

Most recently, Arun accepted a position as senior vice president and CFO of a high-tech spinoff that is 75% owned by the company and 25% by a leading software entity. He is the most experienced person in senior management; his job is to shepherd the new venture – and its young managers – until market conditions are right for it to go public or be sold. When Arun and I talked, market conditions were indicating a sale happening soon, within a few months; he was already casting his net for the next intriguing opportunity.

I asked if he had ever aspired to become CEO and run the company – if the disappointment had been larger than being blocked from the controller position. He responded, "No – because of the time commitment, and the politics. I've never been a 'yes' person. As I've gotten more accustomed to the ways of American companies, I've become reasonably blunt, even with my bosses. That's probably been a hindrance. I remember an experience with a group president for whom I worked. He wanted to spend money not in the budget and hide the expenditure from corporate management. To me that's just not ethical in business – so I prepared the financial projection as it should have been, showing the expenditure, and was very clear with everyone what we were doing. My boss was very unhappy about that. Those kinds of things have not helped me, but at the end of the day you go home and if you don't have integrity and you don't feel good about yourself, what do you have?"

The Bigger Picture

Sorting through the experiences of Lynn, Ron, and Arun, we can identify several important questions you need to ask yourself in order to walk the talk on money and success. The questions are:

> How ambitious are you? If you're hard-wired to be a significant achiever, fine; the world needs you. Be sure that your drive comes from inside, and not from someone else's expectations snapping at your heels. Be sure you're honest with the people who love you about how much of your time and emotional energy will be left over for them.

How much do you rely on external signals to bolster your self-esteem, as opposed to relying on an inner sense of accomplishment? If you need the external markers that larger work systems provide – a career ladder to climb, pay scales, perks – you probably need to stay in a setting where those things are available. Even though the politics or slow decision making in big systems may make you unhappy, be honest with yourself about how you'd really feel about working on your own or in a smaller system without established ways to keep score.

How important is intimacy in your life, especially as it regards children, a spouse or partner, or significant other? This is a really tough one to be honest about. Recently I had lunch with a colleague whose younger son is in middle school and playing sports. With her heavy work-related travel schedule, she is really unable to do anything else in her life other than work and family obligations, and feels as if she's missing a lot in terms of things she'd like to do for herself. Kate Bruce, a psychotherapist quoted earlier in the book, also has a son in middle school and one in high school, both of whom play baseball. From May until October, Kate is on the sidelines for almost every game, content to schedule client appointments that allow for a 4 P.M. departure from the office so that she can arrive at the game by the second or third inning. These two women have very different feelings when it comes to juggling income, opportunities for professional success, self-care, and time to deepen intimacy.

Which variation on the provider/organizer model best suits your temperament and relationships? Take a careful look at your situation now, and pick the closest fit with one of the models described in Chapter 5. If changing your relationship to money and success will alter the model – either at home or at work – you'll have to negotiate that change with whomever you share provider/organizer responsibilities.

What does a "secure platform from which to launch a dramatic life change" look life for you? This is about taking time to gather yourself and create a secure platform before you make a move, so that you're able to assess what really might be a better direction. People who simply rebound reflexively from situations that make them unhappy are unlikely to find contentment. They're more likely to land in deeper turmoil and confusion.

How big a professional footprint you need to make in order to feel successful? There are lots of things in the world that are worthwhile doing – some of them make a big and visible mark, and others are more quietly meaningful. If you need "big, public, and visible" to be really happy, you need to channel your drive for money and success in that direction. If not, you can allow for more variation in your choices.

What price will you pay to rise to the top? In a previous chapter we talked about the "right, wrong, and relative of money." As you climb the ladder in large work systems, you get a lot more complicated "right, wrong, and relative" moments to deal with, and the consequences are often huge. You have to know what "integrity at the end of the day" means to you going in, because the pace of work moves too quickly these days for you to learn on the job. When you weigh making a move, you have to be very clear about what will be required of you in order to achieve success, and ask yourself if it's a price you are willing to pay.

From my experience working with clients over the last ten years, I'd add these additional points for you to keep in mind.

Making a voluntary change in your relationship with money and success doesn't usually "just happen." For most people, it's the culmination of a deliberate, intentional process. When I begin to see a new client, I typically ask that person how he or she came to be working in a particular profession or in a certain kind of work system. Much more often than I would have anticipated, the answer is something like, "I sort of just fell into it. The job was there and the pay and benefits were good enough, so I signed on – not necessarily intending to stay. Over time I found I liked the work, so I got more education and continued in the field, and pretty soon it became a career." Making a significant change in your relationship with money and success – one that you initiate, not one that's forced on you by downsizing or a withdrawn offer – is different. Making a decision to walk the talk usually begins with a nagging sense that something about your professional life isn't quite right, even if your situation is the envy of all. You may try to brush the thought away, telling yourself, "What's not to like? I have a great job, I'm making terrific money, I have tons of control over what I do, and I get all kinds of recognition. What more could anyone expect? Maybe I've just been driving too hard and need a weekend away." The point at which you can say, "Even though my situation looks perfect from the outside, I'm not happy. I need to take a look at this," is the point at which the deliberate process begins.

A renegotiation with your money and your success is as apt to happen in a climate of high achievement as in a work situation that's failing. This is a situation where cultural or familial messages about "should" and "ought" can really get you into trouble. Common wisdom says that if things are going really well, we should be grateful and not tempt fate by making changes. The problem with common wisdom in this case is simple. There's no "should" when it comes to happiness. Happiness is a feeling, which can be present, possible but unrecognized, or missing. A big part of happiness is a sense of "fit" between you and the world around you. If you don't have that sense of fit, you're probably not happy and need to consider a change – even if a legion of others would give a lot to be where you are, and even if you hear voices in the background telling you you're an ungrateful wretch.

Changing your relationship to money and success calls for the world view of a tinkerer, not a conformist. People who "tinker" tend to be more curious about what's out there in the world and what else can work than they are fearful about being an outsider to the tribe. Ron actually used the word "tinker" in describing his change. "Before I left the law firm, I didn't pretend to have a fully developed business and personal life plan. I only had the best confidence I could attain that my business plan was operationally and financially feasible, and its implications for my personal life offered some promise of improvement. I was content with this because what I was really after was the freedom to tinker. Importantly, I would have that freedom precisely because I and my family – and not my law partners – would bear the risks and rewards of my forays into the unknown. I knew I could never give myself that freedom within the more structured confines of my obligations to the law firm."

"Platform to launch" may be less formidable a requirement than you think. Earlier, I said that most of us need a secure platform from which to launch ourselves into a new way of acting. When you hear the word "platform," you may be thinking of something really massive. As you consider changing your relationship to money and success, you may worry that you don't have a secure enough base even to think about moving in a different direction. Actually, that's not what "platform to launch" has to mean. Let me give you an analogy from indoor rock climbing, a sport I began when I turned 50. Rock climbing, like changing your relationship to money, is very inner-directed; there are no cheering crowds likely to be waving you on. Rock climbing is also highly skill-driven; you get much, much better with practice. As a

beginner, you need big, clunky, obvious outcroppings of rock to grab as handholds and footholds while you ascend. As you gain skill, you can find a secure enough handhold or foothold in tinier and tinier slivers of rock. From a distance, it might look as if you're ascending an almost sheer face. "Platform to launch" means only that: a secure enough point in your life (whatever "secure enough" means to you right now) where you can safely pause just long enough to shift direction. The platform doesn't even have to be visible to others.

You can't launch and hold on at the same time. You can easily get to the top of a beginner climbing wall keeping three points of contact with the wall at all times and stretching the other hand or foot until you grasp the next hold. I was astonished to find that you can't scale an advanced wall that way. You have to plot your ascent carefully. Then, in order to keep moving up, there will come a point at which you have to let go of two or even three points of contact with the wall. For an instant, it's like being poised in thin air. Then, counter to the pull of gravity, you thrust your body upward or sideways to grab the next set of holds. The sensation is breathtaking. Changing your relationship to money and success is much like that. You have to plot your course, and come up with a reasonable plan. Then, when you're ready, you have to let go of what you know – move counter to the pull of all the built-up expectations that hold you where you are – and go for it. The exhilaration of cutting yourself loose can simultaneously leave you breathless and give you a big shot of momentum.

Know that to move through life at the peak of your ability is to fall. The goal is not to avoid falling, but to master how to fall and recover without hurting yourself. This is the hardest point for compulsive overachievers to absorb. I'm not talking about learning to forgive yourself for failures. I'm talking about building into your expectation that knowing how to work through failure is part of peak performance. Again, the analogy is with rock climbing, this time outdoors. In February 1996 *The Atlantic* carried an article about Dan Osman, a world-class climber who has mastered the ability to fall at the end of a climbing rope from a height of 660 feet without decapitating himself or cutting his body in two from the jolt at the bottom. Why would anyone even want to master such a skill? Think about it: to climb higher and still be safe, you have to know how to fall farther and still be safe.

To really "walk the talk" on money and success and values, you'll find yourself coming up against incredibly challenging situations. Some you'll handle well, others not. To keep moving forward, you have to master the ability to fall, rebound, and find your footing again. You have to master falling to continue succeeding with your climb.

Getting Started

A friend and colleague called to ask if we might find time to have dinner. She is a stellar building principal, and has been told she is being groomed for the superintendency of the district – an appointment to be made sooner rather than later. If the district were to put resources into preparing her, they would count on her accepting the position when the time came. The decision loomed large, and she was groping for a way to get her arms around all the factors she needed to consider. As we began to compare calendars, I asked her two questions about ambition. "How passionate are you about initiating really big changes – the kind that only a superintendent can launch? And, what are you willing to give up in the rest of your life to wield that power?" Curiously enough, just as her excitement about the prospect of leading a school district grew, she was thrown a curve ball. The superintendent unexpectedly complicated the picture by naming another district principal as his assistant, giving that individual a potential advantage in any future search process. At that point, my friend was forced to make the possibility of becoming a superintendent her own career goal – not something to be offered or withheld by her current boss.

"Walking the talk" is often a difficult and costly process involving really hard choices. Yet the process can begin with a simple, almost casual question. "At the end of the day, what do you really want to be doing?" Walking the talk, which has everything to do with happiness, means just this: going forward with what we profess to value and believe, despite the often-significant cost.

Conclusion
"Happiness Is . . ."

Cynthia Winton-Henry, the minister, dancer, and change agent quoted earlier in the book, thinks the most important thing to carry is one's life purpose. My life purpose is to be a story catcher, and I like catching money stories the best. Money stories are the ones least told.

Money stories are about people and organizations exercising the power of choice. Choices about money – steps we put into action – reveal us to ourselves and to the world in very tangible ways. Our choices show what we value, believe, fear, long for, reject, what we most deeply need in order to feel safe, and what our organizations need in order to thrive.

We make money choices every day. When you stitch together all those instances, you get someone's story. When you stitch together all the individual stories, you get the shared money story of a family, a company, an organization, a system of educators or healers, an agency, a faith community, a law-making body, or a people.

Stories need to be put into words so that they can be told and retold, so that we can learn from experience and mentor others. Our stories tell us, again and again, who we are and what we care about. Stories matter; stories are the glue that holds our psyches and spirits together. Stories are the sturdy platform from which we push off and go out into the world. Stories, in a business sense, create our brand. Stories sustain the longings and dreams that beckon people and organizations into the future.

For successful people, money stories go right to the issue of happiness. As I paraphrase three of the people you've met in earlier chapters of the book, you'll hear echoes of their voices:

"If I have all this money, all these choices, all this recognition, why am I not happy? I really thought I would be."

"If my company has delivered real value to our shareholders and customers, why do I feel so disappointed, as if it's still not enough, as if I'm not yet able to feel contented with myself?"

"If I've treated over 30,000 patients during ten years of practice and achieved financial independence at this rather young age, am a good husband and father and son, why do I still feel that my life is insignificant?"

The persistence of these questions demonstrates a simple truth: money and success, in and of themselves, don't add up to happiness. There's a missing piece. Money tells us, in stark and measurable ways, what we really care about – or what our organizations value. On an individual level, we then have the challenge of making what we care about, say, and do all fit together. On an organizational level, we face the challenge of making what the organization proclaims as its mission and values congruent with what gets rewarded.

How do we meet that challenge? We do so by mastering the tools of money literacy:

Identifying our chosen containers

Developing our money autobiography

Figuring out our current money stage

Determining how we use money's power

Negotiating our provider/organizer role

Deciding what we think money is for

Developing some consistent basis for working through the right, wrong, and relative of money

Deciding how much is enough

After mastering these tools, we can then act on what we learn.

Happiness, viewed through the lens of money and success, means the daily practice of walking the talk. That means integrating story and behavior with our deepest beliefs and values. The daily practice never ends.

Joan's technology company was badly destabilized by the business downturn in late 2000 and early 2001 and had to do considerable downsizing. "Capitalism," she told me, "pounds good people and bad people equally. There's no floor under the pain. Telling someone who's done a good job for you that they're out is the worst experience you can have as a business owner. You're admitting there's no bulwark to be found against these larger market forces – whether you're brilliant as a leader or an idiot." Although turbulent markets have also hit their personal investment portfolio, Joan and her husband continue to feel confident that they have enough money for her to continue with the plan to take a year's sabbatical. They sold their home and condo in separate cities and have consolidated their belongings into what Joan refers to as a "vintage Norma Desmond" residence in which they will now live together. Joan sees that step as the culmination of the moment in my office when she and her husband focused on the "money + success = happiness" equation and committed themselves to putting each other and their life together first, not last after all other obligations had been met. That's another facet of happiness: shifting the definition of "what matters most" from external factors to your own inner sense, and finally being able to take your hand off the hot burner.

The pediatric oncologist told me he had made a mistake in thinking that there was a pathway out of his suffering. He's thrown himself back into his medical practice, vastly increasing its size and the demands on his time, energy, and emotions. I told him I could hear the pain in his voice. He responded, "Pain is part of the adventure." There's no entitlement to happiness, even for good and decent souls who long for it. Becoming aware and intentional about our money story doesn't result in a particular outcome – just the outcome we are best able to live with.

Eric has progressed from giving money to causes he supports to asking others for money. That's a big step for him, and one that further integrates money into his daily life. He has come to understand that successful people who serve on nonprofit boards are expected to raise money. He's happiest being who he is, which in this case means doing what people with money do. Coming out publicly as a millionaire at age 60 was harder, he told me, than coming out as gay, which he began to do as a young boy.

> There are lots of parallels in coming out as gay and coming out as a person with money. First you have to come out to yourself, be honest about who you really are. Then, slowly, you come out to others. You reveal yourself more by what you do than by a big announcement. You don't get married or have children. Your friends are mostly other men. You march in the Gay Pride parade. You go to New York every year for Stonewall. You travel to Turkey for two months, with no visible means of support. You get a new car. You stop trying to fit in with your friends by complaining along with them about how hard it is to pay the bills.
>
> There's a risk in showing others who you really are. Sometimes, when people finally see you, they don't like what they see and walk away. Sometimes, if you've lived a lie and pretended to be something you're not, people are angry at having been duped.

Another side of happiness is "breaking through our fears to reveal who we really are and trusting in the outcome."

Two days after Karen, the nurse manager, had her double mastectomy, I visited her in the hospital. Shortly before her scheduled surgery date, the hospital announced it would be closing in ninety days – the victim of overcapacity, falling reimbursements, bad management decisions, and ruthless competition for market share among area hospitals. People on the verge of losing their jobs and financial security were caring for Karen, for the most part compassionately and well. As I sat by her bed, Karen was not thinking about their plight, although under other circumstances she might well have been empathetic to her fellow health care workers. Nor was she thinking about the bills piling up during her recuperation. In the raw pain of the moment, Karen was thinking only about living and dying. Sometimes money issues are front and center, boldly before our eyes. Sometimes they recede into the background, falling well below our conscious radar. They never go entirely away.

Lynn is successfully juggling her ramped-up corporate career, her marriage, and being a mother to two young children. She's energized and happy with her life. Her husband continues to be the one predictably home for dinner and for emergencies with the kids; she recognizes him as a wonderful father. She surprised me with the news that she is pregnant, expecting their third baby. She'll take three months maternity leave, as she did with her other two infants, and will then return to work with the ongoing support of her full-time nanny. She anticipates no unmanageable difficulty continuing to make it all come together. Her voice is confident and excited. "Despite what I told you about loving my career, I also love being a mom. I love my husband. I love who we are as a family. We're really happy together and we felt that we could support the major decision to have another child. My debut with our corporate-wide board of directors will come when I am seven months pregnant. I'm thinking about how rare it is that these men – the directors are almost all men – look up and see a very pregnant woman delivering the marketing strategy for the whole corporation. I'm a lot of things in my life, and that makes me really happy. I'm the mom delivering my son to soccer in our van, and I'm also the corporate vice president of marketing delivering strategy to our board." Happiness is being able to relish the times when life, with all its conflicting and competing demands, is much better than you could have dared to hope.

Ron has just raised his hourly rate, having no shortage of clients who are demanding of his time. He also took a weekday off to accompany his twelve-year-old daughter on her school's "outdoor education" day for kids and their parents, something he would never have done as head of a corporate law group. Most recently he and his daughter had not been seeing eye-to-eye, and he didn't know if their spending the day together was a good idea. As it turned out, she was elated to have her father with her for a whole day. His daughter's joy affirmed Ron's importance in her life and made him feel happy beyond words, even ecstatic. "Running around a camp with a bunch of kids, one of whom is my daughter and who is, even at age 12, delighted to have her father there and proud that he showed up, that to me is as happy as I can ever get in the world." Happiness is letting yourself have what you most long for and letting that be enough.

What You Do Tells the Tale

Through all their growing-up years, Jerry and I told our kids that whatever they chose to do professionally – as long as it was work they loved and which made them happy – was fine with us. In high school Matt was deeply influenced by a wonderful constitutional law teacher. "Mr. Harrison says . . ." became a nightly part of our family dinner conversation. At one point, Matt asked us how we would feel if he became a teacher like Mr. Harrison. We said – and meant – that it would be fine, reminding Matt that his aunt and uncle are lifelong public school teachers. His now-retired grandaunt taught all six grades in a one-room schoolhouse in rural Iowa. Early in my professional career I had taught young school children with learning disabilities.

What we said and meant was not really what Matt and Sara saw. Jerry and I, each for reasons of our own, have been highly competitive and demanding of ourselves professionally, and intensely focused on creating financial independence. For me, that has been a decision to compensate for the financial anxiety that has been so much a part of my family of origin money story for at least three generations. Jerry's motivation is harder for him to identify. I suspect that part of it is having grown up a bright Jewish boy in a post-World War II culture, where he absorbed the message that the world would not protect his European Jewish forebears and that he would have to shoulder that task for his own family when he became a man. For Jerry, financial security is about feeling safe and feeling in control.

As young adults, Matt and Sara are highly competitive and demanding of themselves. Following her year as the highest producer the travel company has ever had and at the age of 24, Sara was appointed manager of the plum new office among the many that her company opened during 2001. Starting from scratch, she unlocked an empty space, supervised the installation of equipment, hired her first employee, and opened the doors for business. Knowing Sara as I do, I suspect she wanted to have the biggest first day and the biggest first week of any new office that her company had ever opened. At the end of that first week I asked her three questions:

Did the equipment work?

Did your new employee show signs of picking up what you were trying to teach her?

Did you do any business?

With three "yes" answers in response, I assured Sara that she was off to a great start – and carefully avoided mentioning production numbers.

Right out of college, Matt was hired as a junior account executive for the Boston office of an Internet-based multimedia company. In less than a year, he earned three promotions. Finally, just before Matt's 23rd birthday, the company announced a search for a director of sales for all of New England. On the day they interviewed someone from the West Coast with fifteen years' sales experience, Matt asked via email if he could also go to New York and present his vision for the region. Because of what he had accomplished but also, I'm sure, because of his sheer chutzpah, Matt got the job.

I have this message for my now-grown offspring: "Life is a marathon, my loved ones, not a sprint. That's not what you saw, but it's what I now know. At some point, even in the hands of a skilled driver, the most finely tuned racecar can take a turn too fast and spin out. Be mindful of that as you rush forward with your lives."

This culture of success that we share as readers accentuates individual experience, fast-forward time, and future opportunity. The culture minimizes community bonds, a sense of the sacred, and a reverence for the wisdom of the past. When those things no longer work the same way they once did, we look for a different way to mark where we stand. For that different marker, we've chosen money – with its awesome power to create change – and professional success. Currency in some form is nearly universal. Money is tangible, easily measurable, and highly visible. Money works very readily as a scorecard on success. Money drives financial independence.

Using money in that way doesn't mean money replaces family, or God, or heritage stories. Money just replaces one absolutely essential thing family and religion and history used to do better than they do now. Money helps you figure out who and where you are in relation to others and in relation to your own aspirations.

Should we grant money that enlarged function?

Money does the "locator" role very well, at least in measuring our relative ability to maximize the economic system. That's a broad talent, not a narrow one. Successful people not only work hard, they also inspire trust. They get people who control opportunities to spot their potential and send interesting projects their way. They attract loyal followers. They take stands and risk stepping apart from the crowd. They set a high performance bar for themselves and for others.

In that sense, money is a very good marker for who's who in the culture of success. Making money isn't bad, tainted, something that needs to be balanced out by less venal pursuits, or a topic to be shielded from polite conversation.

Money is a good marker, but not a unique or sufficient one. Money needs to be joined by other markers that take account of aspects of human experience that we value but can't so easily quantify. Being known as someone people can count on might be one example. Being able to express empathy might be another.

What's "Enough"?

"Enough," in the simplest sense, is finding what you most need and having it last as long as you need it.

While I was writing this book, and without my knowledge, an aunt that I had not seen in many years was dying of emphysema at her home in Florida. The second youngest of my mother's nine siblings, Dotty was sharp, angular, and edgy. She could be gay and witty, then turn on a dime to be cruel and demeaning. She was never an easy person. She held grudges. She and a favorite niece had words ten or fifteen years ago; they have rarely seen each other and have spoken only sporadically since. Dotty started smoking in the 1940s, when it was a sign of sophistication for a woman to drag on a cigarette. Divorced after less than a year of marriage, Dotty took her infant son, moved back in with my grandmother, put on stockings and high heels and "went to business" as a supervisor for the phone company. Our mothers mostly wore pink shirtwaist dresses and flats and kept house in those days; the cousins and I all thought Dotty was the most glamorous of the aunts. We hardly ever saw her without a cigarette. She smoked two or three packs a day for over thirty years and then stopped – but the damage was done.

Dotty lived the last decades of her life at a great geographical and emotional distance from family. She quarreled with some siblings, and simply stopped seeing or speaking with others and with most of her nieces and nephews. She married again; her husband Russell thought she looked like a movie star and treated her as such. Between her pension from the phone company and his from General Motors, they had good health care, enough money, the Florida sun, and each other as company. My cousin Greg moved in and out of his mother's life, having no contact with her at all for years at a time. At the time when Dotty's emphysema became end-stage, neither my sisters nor I had seen her for almost twenty years, and Greg for longer than that.

Wendy, my younger sister, has a good and generous heart. When she and her husband were using our rented condominium in Florida, Wendy told me she was going to take time to drive the hour and a half to visit Dotty – something I had carefully avoided doing. Wendy found Dotty on oxygen in her mobile home, acutely ill and in need of emergency care. Once in the hospital, Dotty asked Wendy to serve as her health care proxy and as executor for the estate. Dotty had no one else, her husband having died, and Greg being missing for many years with no family contact at all. Wendy agreed.

Before deciding to leave corporate America and becoming a successful consultant, Wendy was an executive for almost twenty-five years. Her project management skills are finely honed. Getting Dotty's legal affairs in order, seeing to the disposition of the mobile home, starting the search for Greg, and helping Dotty consider options for what was expected to be the last six months of her life took Wendy relatively little time. Over a period of about three weeks, Wendy traveled back and forth between New Jersey and Florida, helping Dotty resolve her affairs. With Wendy there to take over the burdens, Dotty's health began to decline very rapidly – the expected six months became "within a few days."

The night before she died, Dotty was able to tell Wendy she felt afraid and to ask that Wendy stay with her. Wendy stayed all night, rubbing Dotty's back, massaging her feet, simply being there when Dotty opened her eyes and tried to say a few words through the oxygen mask.

Money is always present in our lives, sometimes in the foreground, sometimes receding into the background. Money bought Dotty excellent health care and the best medication and technology available to patients with end-stage pulmonary disease. She didn't have to struggle to breathe in a single-room-occupancy hotel, alone and with the bathroom down the hall. Money gave Dotty the ability to pay Wendy's expenses and to buy the kinds of legal and other services Wendy needed to resolve the affairs rapidly. Having the money for Wendy to go back and forth mattered immensely, and set up the final, significant moment, the answer – for both of them – to "what's enough?" That moment went beyond the power of money and reached for those aspects of human experience that we value but can't so easily quantify.

At the end of her life and much weakened from her usual flinty manner, Dotty allowed herself to risk what she had too often pushed away: the comfort of another human being. Dotty told Wendy she was afraid to die alone, and asked Wendy to stay. In a niece with a caring heart – although in large measure a stranger to her as an adult – Dotty found the response she most needed, and it lasted all the way until the end. In the morning Dotty was transferred to the hospice unit. With morphine relieving her suffering she died later that day, with Wendy still at her side.

Money serves a large and significant role in the culture of success, and is a vital lens through which we can see our way to happiness. We also need honest conversation about what else is important – or needs to be. That will vary from person to person. What will not vary is that the pursuit of money can be central in our experience, but shouldn't stand on center stage alone.

Money Autobiography

Name _____ Current age _____

Occupation _____

In your own words, how would you describe your current level of financial security:

_____

_____

_____

Money Autobiography is a tool for helping you tell significant events in your life from the perspective of money. For many of us, money serves as a "silent subtext" to current events and relationships. As long as money stays silent it's hard to make good use of what we know, and hard to get a handle on money's transforming power. If you can become more intentional about your relationship with money, you have a much better chance of being able to use money to get what you want in your personal and professional life.

The following questions are designed to help you get started. If you find your story going in a different direction from that suggested by the questions, follow your own direction.

Family of Origin

Your earliest learning about money, how it's used, what it can and can't do, came from your family of origin. It's important to know what information and experiences you started with.

1. Did your father work outside the home? At what? Do you know how much he earned? How do you know? Was money openly discussed in your family?
2. Aside from the effects of inflation, do you earn more or less than your father did at a comparable age?
3. Do you know what your father wanted you to be professionally? Do you know if he's happy with what you did become?
4. Did your mother work outside the home? At what? Do you know how much she earned? How do you know? Do you earn more or less than she did at a comparable age? If she didn't work outside the home, did she have anything to do with the way family money was handled?
5. Do you know what your mother wanted you to be professionally? Do you know if she's happy with what you did become?

Current Money Skills

Money has both a literal and a symbolic meaning. These questions ask about the literal side of handling money.

1. How skilled do you consider yourself at the basics of money management? Do you keep pretty good track of your finances? Do you understand how financial instruments like mutual funds, retirement plans, etc., work? Do you have a basic grasp of financial principles, like "the time value of money"?
2. How did you acquire whatever level of skill you have? At what age did that learning process begin? Who was instrumental in helping you learn?
3. How would you describe your risk tolerance? Are there any important life events that have affected how much risk you are willing or able to take?

Your Money Story

The purpose here is to tell significant events of your life from the perspective of money. The goal is to get at the symbolic meaning of money, at the way money "stands in" for deeper psychological experiences. You don't have to answer the questions sequentially, or respond to every one. Use the questions as a guide for getting you started. Remember to follow your own instincts about what's important as you tell your story. Don't hesitate to write about something even if it's not covered by one of the questions.

1. What's the first time you remember having money? What did you do with it? Did someone else tell you what you had to do with all or part?
2. What's the first time you remember earning money? How free were you to decide what to do with it? What did you do?
3. Has money ever made a significant difference in a relationship?
4. Have you ever seen money used to control another person or situation? Have you ever used money in that way?
5. What do you think money has to do with professional success? How much of what you think is governed by messages you got from people you care about? How much stems from messages conveyed by the overall culture?
6. In your current family system, who's "the provider"? How does that affect daily decision making? In other words, how does that affect who gets to call the shots?
7. Do you talk openly about money in your current family system? What money issues are easiest to talk about? Hardest?
8. Have you had to juggle work and family issues, that is, balance your career aspirations with the needs of small children, elderly parents, a spouse/partner who also works? What role does money play in that balancing act?
9. Did money have anything to do with your choice of life partner?
10. Do you feel entitled to make or inherit or win a lot of money? Why or why not?
11. How would you describe your values with respect to money? Where did those values come from? If you sat down with your checkbook and credit card bills, would the way you actually spend money fit with your values?
12. If you have more money than you need, do you give charitably? Why or why not? Do you support political figures? Why or why not? Do you look for ways to leverage your assets by investing, backing new business ideas, etc.? Why or why not?
13. Beyond your home and car, what's the largest amount of money you've ever spent on yourself? What did you buy?
14. Do you have any spiritual or religious beliefs that affect your use of money? If so, please describe. If not, what helps you determine how you use money?
15. In the end, what does money do for you? What does it not do?

Your Central Money Drama

Often there's a central theme or ongoing drama around money that you can "see" once you've completed the questions. Examples of such central themes include "having and losing," or "never enough," or "pretending that money doesn't really matter, but it does."

1. As you read back over what you've written, can you identify your central money drama?
2. How does that drama affect you on a day-to-day basis, in terms of your choices about where to focus your energies?
3. How would you like that drama to change?
4. If you could harness the power of your money in more positive ways, what would that look like?
5. If you felt secure in your financial situation, what would you do differently, and how do you hope it would feel?

INDEX